THE DEATH OF DEPOSITS

THE DEATH OF DEPOSITS

How Banks Can Turn the $124 Trillion Wealth Transfer into Their Greatest Opportunity

Martha Sylla Underwood

Published by Underwood Holdings, Birmingham, AL

The stories of Margaret Chen, Jennifer Chen, Sarah Martinez, and other individuals depicted in this book are composite narratives based on common patterns in estate settlement. Names, identifying details, and specific circumstances are fictional. The systemic challenges depicted reflect documented industry practices, regulatory requirements, and publicly available research. Any resemblance to actual persons, living or deceased, is coincidental.

Case illustrations, financial projections, and institutional examples throughout this book are intended for educational and analytical purposes. They do not constitute financial, legal, or regulatory advice. Readers should consult qualified professionals regarding their specific circumstances.

ISBN: 978-1-953653-16-1
First Edition

Printed in the United States of America

For every family navigating the worst week of their lives,
and for the bankers who choose to show up for them.

ACKNOWLEDGMENTS

To my sons, KJ and Kole, who I build for every day. Everything I do starts and ends with you.

To my parents Marc, Marie, and my siblings that sustains me, you've always pushed me higher and didn't let me settle. You celebrated every small win and reframed every setback as a setup. The standard you hold me to isn't about perfection. It's about purpose. And I deeply appreciate it.

To the banking executives, estate professionals, and families who shared their experiences with me, you let me see the problem clearly enough to write about it honestly. This book exists because you trusted me. Special thanks to Mitch Waycaster, Jeff Murphy, Mark Williams, Stan Viner, Jeff McCormack, Bob Dickerson, and Willie Bass for their insight, candor, and belief in what this work represents.

To Seth Godin, whose thinking on the courage it takes to see what others refuse to name has shaped how I approach every hard conversation, including the ones in this book.

To the team at Prismm, building something that matters requires people who believe it matters. And you do, every day.

To Kent, for being present during the years this was written.

Martha

CONTENTS

CHAPTER ONE

The Day Your Best Customer Dies

Margaret Chen had been a customer of First Community Bank for forty-three years.

She opened her first account there in 1983, the same year she and her husband David bought their house on Maple Street. Over the decades, she'd celebrated promotions with larger deposits, weathered recessions, and watched her balance grow from a few thousand dollars to just over $847,000 in savings, CDs, and a money market account. She knew three generations of tellers by name. When the bank installed its first ATM, Margaret was skeptical. When they launched mobile banking, she was one of the first seniors to download the app.

Margaret died on a Tuesday in October. She was seventy-eight.

Her daughter, Jennifer, found herself standing in the bank's lobby the following Friday, clutching a manila folder containing her mother's death certificate, the will naming her as executor, and a handwritten list of account numbers she'd discovered in a kitchen drawer. Jennifer had taken the day off work. She assumed this would take an hour, maybe two.

It would take eleven months.

The Call No One Prepared For

The first thing Jennifer learned was that the bank couldn't tell her anything. Not the balances. Not which accounts existed. Not even whether her mother had a safe deposit box. The teller, a young woman who clearly wished she were somewhere else, explained that Jennifer would need to speak with "Estate Services," which was apparently a single person in a regional office forty miles away, available by appointment only, with the next opening in three weeks.

"But I'm the executor," Jennifer said, holding up the will. "It says right here."

"I understand, ma'am. But we need to verify everything with the probate court first."

Jennifer drove home in a fog. Her mother had been meticulous about her finances. She'd paid off the mortgage in 2011, kept six months of expenses in her checking account, and invested the rest conservatively. She'd even written a letter, found in the same kitchen drawer, explaining where everything was and what Jennifer should do.

What Margaret couldn't have known, what no amount of preparation could have anticipated, is that her bank had no system for what came next.

The Volume Nobody Talks About

Jennifer Chen's story isn't unusual. It's, in fact, becoming the most common customer journey in American banking, and the one that financial institutions are least prepared to handle.

The math is simple. And it should keep you up at night.

According to the U.S. Census Bureau, approximately 10,000 Baby Boomers have been crossing the age-65 threshold every day since 2011. By 2030, every member of this generation, all 73 million Americans born between 1946 and 1964, will be at least 65 years old. The oldest Boomers turned 80 in 2026.

But crossing into retirement age isn't the crisis. The crisis is what comes after.

The National Center for Health Statistics reports that the United States experiences approximately 2.8 million deaths annually. This baseline, roughly 7,700 deaths per day, has been relatively stable for years. What's changing is the composition. As the massive Boomer generation moves through its seventies and into its eighties, the proportion of deaths occurring among this cohort is accelerating dramatically. Census Bureau projections show annual deaths rising to 3.6 million by 2037 and continuing to climb as the generation ages through peak mortality years.

To put this in banking terms: every single day, thousands of deposit accounts, investment relationships, safe deposit boxes, and lending relationships require some form of death-related processing. Every day, families arrive at branches with death certificates, looking for guidance. Every day, assets sit frozen while paperwork moves through systems designed for an era when this volume was a fraction of what it's today.

And we haven't even talked about the money yet.

$124 Trillion in Motion

Cerulli Associates, the wealth management research firm, has been tracking what they call the "Great Wealth Transfer" for over a decade. Their most recent projections, published in late 2024, estimate that $124 trillion in assets will change hands through 2048.

Take a moment with that number.

That figure is more than five times the annual GDP of the United States. It represents the accumulated wealth of the most prosperous generation in human history, equity in homes purchased when a middle-class salary could afford a middle-class house, retirement accounts that benefited from the longest bull market in American history, and savings accumulated across decades of economic growth.

Of that $124 trillion, approximately $100 trillion, 81 percent, will transfer from Baby Boomers and their surviving Silent Generation parents to younger heirs or to charity. More than half of these transfers will flow from households currently classified as high-net-worth or ultra-high-net-worth, meaning they hold at least $1 million in investable assets.

But here's the detail that should concern every bank executive reading this: Millennials are projected to inherit $46 trillion, more than any other generation. Gen X will receive $39 trillion. Gen Z will ultimately inherit $15 trillion.

These are generations that grew up with Venmo and Robinhood. They hold their primary checking accounts at digital banks. They consider a branch visit an anachronism. And the moment they inherit their parents' assets, they will be deciding whether to leave that money where it sits, at your institution, or move it somewhere else.

The research is clear: you should be worried. Studies consistently show that inherited assets are among the most mobile in all of financial services. The friction of moving money, once a reliable retention mechanism, has collapsed. A beneficiary can open an account at a digital competitor and initiate a transfer in minutes.

The real question: Will your institution give them a reason to stay?

What Actually Happens

Let's return to Jennifer Chen, because her experience illustrates the systemic failures that most banks have normalized.

Week 1: Jennifer contacts the bank. She's told to wait for the estate services appointment. In the meantime, automatic bill payments continue to drain her mother's checking account, payments for a cell phone Margaret no longer needs, subscriptions to magazines she'll never read. Jennifer can't stop them.

Week 3: The estate services appointment occurs. Jennifer learns she needs "Letters Testamentary" from the probate court before the bank can do anything. She had assumed the will itself was sufficient. It wasn't. The bank representative is polite but clearly reciting from a script. No one asks how Jennifer is doing. No one offers condolences.

Week 8: Jennifer receives Letters Testamentary from the court. She returns to the bank, where she's told the documents need to be reviewed by the legal department. Processing time: 7-10 business days.

Week 10: Legal review is complete. Jennifer can now see her mother's account balances. She can't, however, transfer funds to the estate account she's opened, at the same bank, because the estate account was opened at a different branch and the systems don't talk to each other.

Week 14: Jennifer returns again, this time with a notarized letter of instruction. The funds are transferred. She asks about the safe deposit box. There's one. She can't access it without a separate appointment and a probate court order, even though she's already been confirmed as executor.

Week 18: Safe deposit box finally opened. Inside: the deed to the house, her parents' marriage certificate, some old coins of uncertain value, and a handwritten note from her father to her mother, dated 1979. Jennifer cries in the vault room. The bank employee stands there, unsure what to do.

Week 23: All liquid assets are finally consolidated. Jennifer begins the process of distributing funds according to the will. Her brother lives in another state and wants his share deposited into his account at a different bank. Wire transfer fees apply. Jennifer is exhausted.

Week 44: The estate is finally closed. Jennifer has visited the bank eleven times. She's spent approximately forty hours on phone calls, paperwork, and appointments. She's paid $487 in various fees. She's had the same conversation with different employees at least eight times because no one had a record of the previous interactions.

In the end, Jennifer moves her own accounts to a different institution. Not because she's angry, though she is, but because every interaction with First Community Bank now reminds her of the worst year of her life.

She takes her $312,000 in personal assets with her.

Her brother never opens an account at First Community at all. He deposits his inheritance at his existing bank.

The $847,000 that Margaret Chen spent forty-three years building at First Community Bank is gone within twelve months of her death.

The Retention Illusion

Ask most bank executives about their customer retention rates and they'll cite impressive numbers, often in the 90th percentile. They'll show you dashboards tracking churn, attrition, and lifetime value.

What they probably can't tell you is what happens to deposits when account holders die.

This isn't a gap in reporting, it's a gap in thinking. Most financial institutions treat death as an exception, an edge case, something that happens occasionally and can be managed by a small team of specialists. Their retention models assume customers leave because of pricing, service failures, or competitor offers. The models don't account for the reality that a substantial and growing portion of customer departures aren't departures at all, they're deaths.

And what happens after death isn't measured as retention. It's not measured as anything.

Consider: if First Community Bank tracked "beneficiary retention" the percentage of inherited assets that stay with the institution, what would that number be? 50 percent? 30 percent? Most banks have no idea. They know they lost Margaret Chen as a customer. They likely coded the account closure as "deceased." End of story.

But Margaret's story wasn't the end. It was a beginning, the beginning of a relationship with Jennifer and her brother, both of whom were potential customers for the next forty years. First Community didn't lose one customer. They lost three.

Now multiply that by 7,700. Every day.

The System Nobody Built

Here is the truth that this book will force into the open: the American financial system wasn't designed to transfer wealth at scale.

Probate law varies by state, fifty different jurisdictions with fifty different rules for small estates, survivor rights, and documentation requirements. Banks operate on legacy systems built for account maintenance, not estate administration. Customer service training covers how to open accounts and handle disputes, not how to navigate grief. Compliance frameworks focus on fraud prevention, which creates a default posture of suspicion toward the very families trying to access inherited assets.

None of this is malicious. It's simply the accumulated weight of systems that evolved for a different era, an era when deaths were less frequent, estates were simpler, and customers didn't have alternatives.

That era is ending.

The generation of bank executives who will navigate this transition, many of whom are Boomers themselves, face a choice. They can continue treating death processing as a cost center, an operational nuisance to be handled as efficiently as possible. Or they can recognize it for what it actually is: the single most important moment in determining whether their institution survives the next two decades.

The Silver Tsunami isn't coming. It's here. The first waves have already crashed against the walls of branch lobbies and call centers across America. The question isn't whether your institution will feel the impact. The question is whether you'll do anything about it before the opportunity disappears.

What This Book Will Show You

In the chapters that follow, we'll dissect why the current system is so broken, the regulatory complexity, the operational tangles, the technology debt that makes change so difficult. We'll examine why beneficiaries leave and where they go. We'll look at the hidden costs that never appear on any balance sheet.

But we'll also chart a path forward.

Because here's what most executives miss: the institution that solves this problem doesn't just retain deposits. It earns the loyalty of an entirely new generation of customers at the exact moment when that loyalty is most valuable. The family that experiences a seamless, compassionate inheritance process doesn't just keep their money with you, they tell their friends, their colleagues, their own children.

The institution that owns the inheritance experience owns the next forty years of that family's financial life.

Margaret Chen was a customer for forty-three years. In a different world, a world where her bank had built the systems, trained the staff, and designed the processes to handle what came next, Jennifer would still be a customer today. Her brother might have opened his first account. Margaret's grandchildren, just now entering the workforce, might have grown up hearing that First Community Bank was there when the family needed them most.

That's not the world we live in. Not yet.

But it could be.

CHAPTER TWO

The 12-Month Hostage Situation

There's a phrase I've heard from families so often that it has come to feel like a diagnosis: "I feel like I'm being held hostage by the bank."

They don't mean it metaphorically. They mean that assets they have a legal right to inherit are sitting in accounts they can't access, accumulating dust while their lives move forward in painful slow motion. They mean that every attempt to resolve the situation seems to generate new requirements, new delays, new reasons why "not yet." They mean that the institution their parent trusted for decades now treats them with a suspicion bordering on hostility.

Understanding how this happens, the specific mechanics of delay, is essential for anyone who wants to fix it. So let's walk through the anatomy of a death claim, step by step, in the kind of detail that most executives never see because it happens far from the C-suite, in branch back offices and call center queues.

What follows is a composite timeline drawn from hundreds of real cases. The details vary, but the pattern is remarkably consistent.

Day 1: The Call

Sarah Martinez's mother died on a Thursday morning in March. By Thursday afternoon, Sarah had begun making calls, to the funeral home, to her mother's doctor, to family members scattered across three states.

On Friday, she called her mother's bank.

"I'm sorry for your loss," said the representative. "Do you have the death certificate?"

Sarah didn't. The funeral home had explained that death certificates take time to process, anywhere from a few days to several weeks, depending on the state and county. In some jurisdictions, the funeral home can expedite the process. In others, families must request certificates directly from the vital records office.

"When you have the death certificate, you'll need to visit a branch in person. We can't discuss the account over the phone."

Sarah asked a reasonable question: Could she at least know which accounts her mother had? Her mother had mentioned a checking account, a savings account, and something about CDs, but Sarah wasn't sure of the details.

"I'm sorry, ma'am. Until we've verified your authority to act on behalf of the estate, we can't provide any account information."

Sarah hung up feeling like she'd done something wrong.

Week 2: The Documents Begin

Sarah received five certified copies of her mother's death certificate, the funeral director had suggested ordering multiple copies, advice that would prove prescient. She also located her mother's will, filed neatly in a folder labeled "Important Papers."

The will was straightforward: Sarah was named executor, and the estate was to be divided equally between Sarah and her brother. Simple enough.

Sarah drove to her mother's bank branch, death certificate and will in hand. She expected this to take an hour or two.

The branch manager was sympathetic but clear: the will wasn't sufficient. Before the bank could grant Sarah access to any information, let alone release any funds, she would need something called "Letters Testamentary."

"What's that?" Sarah asked.

The manager explained that Letters Testamentary is a document issued by the probate court officially authorizing an executor to act on behalf of an estate. Even though the will named Sarah as executor, only the court could formally appoint her and grant her legal authority.

"How long does that take?"

"It varies. Usually a few weeks, sometimes longer."

Sarah left with a photocopy of a form titled "Documentation Requirements for Deceased Account Holders." The list included:

- Certified copy of the death certificate
- Letters Testamentary or Letters of Administration from the probate court
- Completed bank forms for estate processing (available upon issuance of court documents)
- Government-issued photo ID for the executor
- Tax identification number for the estate, known as an Employer Identification Number or EIN

Sarah had assumed that being named in a will was enough. She was beginning to understand that the will was just the beginning.

Week 3 - 4: The Probate Process Begins

Sarah hired a probate attorney. She could have filed the paperwork herself, but the attorney warned that mistakes in the initial filing could cause weeks of delay. The cost: $2,500 as an initial retainer.

Together, they filed a Petition for Probate with the court in the county where Sarah's mother had lived. The petition included the original will, the death certificate, and an application naming Sarah as executor.

Then they waited.

The court's processing time for initial petitions varied depending on the county's caseload. In Sarah's county, the clerk's office was running about three weeks behind. Other families, in other counties, faced backlogs of six to eight weeks, or longer.

Meanwhile, Sarah's mother's bills continued to arrive. The mortgage. The utilities. The credit cards. Sarah had no authority to pay these from her mother's accounts, so she paid them from her own checking account, trusting she'd be reimbursed eventually.

The total, by the end of the first month: $3,847.

Week 6: The Hearing

Six weeks after her mother's death, Sarah attended a probate hearing. It lasted approximately twelve minutes.

The judge reviewed the petition, confirmed the will appeared valid, and formally appointed Sarah as executor. The clerk's office would issue Letters Testamentary within five to seven business days.

Sarah felt, briefly, like she was making progress.

Week 7: Back to the Bank

Armed with her Letters Testamentary (she'd ordered six certified copies at $10 each, per her attorney's advice), Sarah returned to the bank.

She presented her documents to a different branch employee, the manager she'd spoken with previously was on vacation. This employee studied the documents carefully, then excused herself to make a phone call.

Twenty minutes later, she returned.

"Everything looks in order. But we need to send these to our Estate Services department for review. Processing time is seven to ten business days."

"Seven to ten business days? I have the court documents right here."

"I understand, ma'am. It's our policy. The estate department needs to verify the documents and set up your access."

Sarah asked if there was any way to expedite the process. Her mother's mortgage payment was due in ten days.

"I can note in the file that it's urgent."

Week 9: Access Granted (Sort Of)

Eleven business days later, Sarah received a call from the bank's Estate Services department. Her access had been approved. She could now see her mother's account balances and make certain transactions.

She learned that her mother had:

- A checking account with a balance of $12,847
- A savings account with a balance of $34,209
- A 12-month CD with a balance of $50,000 (maturity date: four months away)
- A safe deposit box (contents unknown)

Total liquid assets: approximately $97,000.

Sarah asked about transferring the funds to an estate account.

"You'll need to come into the branch and open an estate checking account. Then you can initiate the transfers."

"Can I do that today?"

"Yes, but you'll need to bring your Letters Testamentary, your personal ID, the death certificate, and the estate's tax identification number."

Sarah had not yet obtained an EIN for the estate. She hadn't realized she needed one.

Week 10: The EIN and the Estate Account

Obtaining an EIN from the IRS took approximately 15 minutes online. This was, genuinely, one of the smoothest parts of the entire process.

Sarah returned to the branch the following day with all required documents. Opening the estate account took approximately 45 minutes.

Then she requested a transfer from her mother's checking account to the new estate account.

"For transfers over $10,000, we need a notarized Letter of Instruction."

"What's that?"

"A document specifying where you want the funds transferred, signed by you as executor and notarized."

Sarah drove to a UPS store, had a one-paragraph letter notarized for $15, and returned to the bank.

The transfer was processed. Three to five business days.

Week 11: The CD Problem

Sarah asked about the CD. Could she cash it out and transfer the funds to the estate account?

"There's an early withdrawal penalty of 180 days of interest. That would be approximately $625."

Sarah considered this. The CD rate was 2.3%. Current savings rates at online banks were approaching 4.5%. The penalty, while annoying, might be worth paying to gain access to the funds.

"I'd like to proceed with the early withdrawal."

"I'll need to submit a request to our Investment Services team. They handle CD liquidations."

"How long will that take?"

"Usually about two weeks."

Sarah asked if there was any way to waive the penalty, given the circumstances. She'd read somewhere that some banks waived early withdrawal penalties upon the death of an account holder.

The employee wasn't sure. She'd have to check.

Three days later, Sarah received a call: No, the penalty couldn't be waived. It was bank policy.

Week 12: The Safe Deposit Box

Sarah asked about the safe deposit box. She knew her mother had one, there was a key in the Important Papers folder, but she had no idea what was inside.

Accessing the box, she learned, required a separate process.

"We need the Letters Testamentary, the death certificate, and we need to schedule an appointment with a manager. Also, depending on the state, we may need to have the box inventoried in the presence of a bank officer."

In some states, the bank is required to inventory the contents of a deceased person's safe deposit box before the executor can remove anything.

This is to protect both the bank and the estate from disputes about what was (or wasn't) in the box.

The next available appointment for box access: three weeks out.

Sarah thought about what might be in that box. Her mother's wedding ring? The deed to the house? Stock certificates? She had no way to know.

Week 15: Inside the Box

The safe deposit box contained:

- The deed to her mother's house (already recorded with the county, but useful to have the original)
- Her parents' marriage certificate
- A life insurance policy from an employer her mother had left twenty years ago (face value: $10,000)
- A small velvet pouch containing her mother's engagement ring and a pair of pearl earrings
- A handwritten letter from Sarah's father, who had died twelve years earlier

Sarah didn't expect the letter. She had not known it existed.

She read it in the bank's vault room while the manager pretended to look at something else. Her father had written it on their 25th wedding anniversary, expressing things he apparently found difficult to say out loud.

Sarah took everything except the letter. That, she held for a long moment before placing it carefully in her purse.

She thanked the manager, who nodded awkwardly, clearly uncomfortable with the emotion in the room.

Week 18: The Life Insurance Complication

Sarah contacted the insurance company listed on the policy she'd found in the safe deposit box. The company had changed names twice since her mother was employed there, but she eventually reached the right department.

The policy was valid. The beneficiary listed was "Estate of Maria Martinez" not Sarah directly.

This meant the $10,000 payout would need to be deposited into the estate account, not paid directly to Sarah. It also meant the insurance company needed copies of the Letters Testamentary, the death certificate, and a completed claim form.

Processing time after document receipt: six to eight weeks.

Week 22: The Mortgage

Five months after her mother's death, Sarah was still managing the mortgage from the estate account. She'd been making payments faithfully, using funds from her mother's accounts.

But now she needed to decide what to do with the house.

Her brother wanted to sell. Sarah was ambivalent, part of her wanted to keep it in the family, but she lived three hours away and couldn't manage a rental property from that distance.

They agreed to sell.

Which raised a new question: Could Sarah sell the house in her capacity as executor? Or did she need additional court authorization?

Her attorney explained that in some states, an executor can sell real property if the will grants them that authority. In other states, court approval is required regardless. In her mother's state, the will did include language authorizing the executor to sell property, but her attorney recommended getting court confirmation anyway, to protect against future challenges.

More paperwork. More waiting.

Week 28: The Sale

The house sold seven months after Maria's death. After paying off the remaining mortgage, real estate commissions, and closing costs, the net proceeds were $247,000.

Those funds were deposited into the estate account.

Sarah now had approximately $340,000 in estate assets ready for distribution.

But she still couldn't distribute anything.

Week 30: The Creditor Claim Period

Sarah's attorney explained that most states require estates to remain open for a minimum period, typically four to six months, to allow creditors to file claims against the estate.

Even if the executor knows of no outstanding debts, the estate must wait out this period. Creditors Sarah didn't know about, medical providers, credit card companies, anyone, had the legal right to file claims.

In her mother's state, the creditor claim period was four months from the date notice was published in the local newspaper.

That notice had been published in Week 8.

The creditor claim period would close in Week 24.

They were past that now. No creditors had filed claims.

But Sarah still needed to file a final accounting with the court before she could close the estate and distribute assets.

Week 35: The Final Accounting

The final accounting is a detailed report showing every financial transaction of the estate: all assets collected, all debts paid, all fees incurred, and the proposed distribution to beneficiaries.

Sarah's attorney prepared the accounting. The court reviewed it. The beneficiaries, Sarah and her brother, signed waivers indicating they had no objection to the accounting or the proposed distribution.

The court approved the accounting. The estate could now be closed.

Total time elapsed: eight months.

Sarah was lucky.

Week 36: The Distribution

Sarah distributed the estate assets: approximately $170,000 to herself, $170,000 to her brother.

Her brother lived in another state. He asked that his share be wired to his account at a national bank.

The estate account was held at a regional bank that charged $35 for outgoing wire transfers.

For a $170,000 transfer, $35 seemed trivial. But something about it bothered Sarah, one more small friction, one more small fee, in a process that had been nothing but friction and fees for eight months.

She paid it.

Week 38: Closing the Estate Account

Sarah returned to the bank one final time to close the estate account.

The balance was $147.23, amounts that had trickled in after the main distribution (a small dividend check, a utility refund).

She transferred the remaining balance to her personal account and closed the estate account.

The bank employee processed the closure, printed a confirmation, and said, "Is there anything else I can help you with today?"

Sarah thought about everything she'd been through. The eleven branch visits. The dozens of phone calls. The documents, the notarizations, the forms.

"No," she said. "I think we're done."

The Decision

Three weeks later, Sarah moved her personal accounts to a different bank.

It wasn't a decision she made consciously, exactly. A friend mentioned that a new online bank was offering a 4.7% savings rate, and Sarah found herself signing up almost automatically.

When the new account was open, she initiated a transfer of her checking balance, $43,000, from her mother's old bank to the new one.

She didn't tell anyone at the old bank she was leaving. She just.. left.

It wasn't anger, exactly. It was something more like exhaustion. Every interaction with that institution now carried the weight of those eight months. The branch lobby, the hold music, even the font on their statements, all of it triggered a low-grade stress response.

She wanted a clean start.

Her brother had never opened an account at their mother's bank. He deposited his inheritance at his existing bank, a large national institution where he'd been a customer for fifteen years.

Between them, Sarah and her brother represented roughly $380,000 in potential deposits, customers who might have stayed for decades, just as their mother had.

The bank that had served their mother for thirty-two years would never see a penny of it.

The Pattern

Sarah's story is neither worst-case nor best-case. It's typical.

The timeline will vary based on state law, estate complexity, and institutional processes. Some estates resolve faster; many take longer. Estates with real property in multiple states, business interests, or family disputes can stretch to two years or beyond.

But the pattern is remarkably consistent:

Phase 1 (Weeks 1 - 6): Documentation and Court Process The family gathers documents, death certificate, will, identification. They file for probate. They wait for court dates and processing. During this phase, the bank can't provide information or release funds.

Phase 2 (Weeks 6 - 12): Bank Processing The executor presents court documents to the bank. The bank reviews, verifies, and processes. Systems are updated. Estate accounts are opened. Transfers are initiated. Each step requires its own timeline.

Phase 3 (Weeks 12 - 24): Asset Management The executor manages estate assets, liquidating investments, selling property, collecting insurance proceeds. Each asset type has its own process and timeline.

Phase 4 (Weeks 24 - 36+): Settlement and Distribution The executor waits out creditor claim periods, prepares final accountings, obtains court approval, and distributes assets. The estate is formally closed.

Throughout this process, the beneficiaries experience the institution not as a helpful partner but as an obstacle to be navigated. The bank's processes, designed for compliance and risk management, create friction at every turn.

And friction, in the age of instant digital transfers, is fatal.

What Banks Don't Track

Here is what most financial institutions don't know about the Sarah Martinezes in their customer base:

They don't know how long the process took. There's no dashboard showing average time-to-resolution for estate cases. No metric tracking the number of branch visits required. No measurement of customer effort.

They don't know how the family felt. No one surveyed Sarah about her experience. No one asked if the process met her expectations. The only feedback mechanism is complaint calls, and most people don't complain, they just leave.

They don't know what happened to the money. When Maria Martinez's accounts were closed, the system recorded a closure due to death. It didn't record that the beneficiaries took their assets to competitors. There's no "beneficiary retention" metric.

They don't know the lifetime value they lost. Sarah is 52 years old. If she lives another 30 years with an average deposit balance of $50,000, that's $1.5 million in deposit-years the bank will never see. Her brother is 48. Add another $1.5 million. The nieces and nephews who might have been introduced to "Grandma's bank"? Uncountable.

The bank that served Maria Martinez for thirty-two years knows only this: she died, her accounts were closed, and the estate was processed according to policy.

They believe they handled it correctly.

They have no idea what they lost.

CHAPTER THREE

The Retention Illusion

Ask any bank executive about their retention rate, and they'll give you a number. It might be 92%. It might be 96%. In credit unions, it's often higher still.

These numbers are presented with pride at board meetings, in investor presentations, and in strategic planning sessions. They suggest stability. They suggest loyalty. They suggest that whatever challenges the institution faces, customer relationships remain strong.

The numbers are accurate. They're also meaningless.

Because buried in that retention rate is a statistical ghost, a category of departure that doesn't register as attrition at all. When a customer dies, their accounts close. The system records this as an "account closure due to death" or "deceased account." It doesn't record it as customer attrition. It certainly doesn't track what happens to the money.

This is the retention illusion: the belief that your retention metrics reflect reality, when in fact they systematically exclude the single largest category of wealth transfer in your institution's history.

What We Don't Measure

Let me pose a simple question: What percentage of inherited deposits leave your institution within 12 months of the original account holder's death?

If you're like most bank executives I've worked with, you don't know the answer. Not because you're negligent, but because your systems weren't designed to track it. The data exists, somewhere, scattered across account opening records, closure codes, transfer logs, and beneficiary databases, but it has never been assembled into a coherent picture.

Here's what the industry research tells us, even if your internal data doesn't:

80% of heirs change financial advisors at the point of inheritance. This statistic, cited repeatedly in wealth management research, should alarm anyone who believes their customer relationships transfer automatically to the next generation. They don't. The relationship was with the deceased, not with the heir.

70% of widows switch financial institutions within a year of their spouse's death. This finding from McKinsey has been replicated across multiple studies. The spouse, who should be the easiest relationship to retain, since they were already part of the household, leaves anyway. And they leave not because of poor investment performance, but because they never felt the institution understood or valued them.

When children inherit, retention drops further. U.S. advisors report retaining relationships 78% of the time when a spouse inherits, but only 58% of the time when children inherit. That 20-point gap represents trillions of dollars flowing to competitors.

46% of financial advisors worldwide consider the Great Wealth Transfer an "existential threat" to their business. They understand what's coming. They're measuring it. They're worried.

These statistics come from the wealth management industry, advisors managing portfolios, not deposit accounts. But the dynamics are identical. An heir who switches investment advisors is the same heir who switches banks. The relationship rupture happens across all financial touchpoints simultaneously.

The Cascade Effect

When inherited assets leave, they don't leave alone.

Consider what happens when a beneficiary has a negative experience settling an estate at their parent's bank:

The inherited deposits leave. This is the obvious loss, the $200,000 checking balance, the $500,000 in CDs, whatever the deceased held at the institution.

The beneficiary's existing relationship leaves. If the beneficiary already had accounts at the same institution, those accounts often follow. Why would they maintain a relationship with an institution that made their worst month even worse?

The extended family leaves. The beneficiary's spouse. Their adult children. Anyone who heard the horror stories over holiday dinners. Reputational damage radiates outward through family networks.

Future referrals never arrive. Every satisfied customer generates referrals over time. Every dissatisfied customer generates anti-referrals, warnings to friends and family to avoid the institution. The beneficiary who spent eleven months fighting for their inheritance becomes a walking cautionary tale.

The lifetime value compounds. A 52-year-old beneficiary who leaves might have remained a customer for another 30 years, with an average balance of $75,000. That's $2.25 million in deposit-years, gone. Multiply by two siblings, and you've lost $4.5 million in potential deposits from a single estate, not including their spouses, children, or referral networks.

This is the cascade that retention metrics don't capture. The death of one customer becomes the departure of five or ten. The closure of one account becomes the loss of a family's financial relationship for generations.

Why We Don't Track It

The failure to measure beneficiary retention isn't malicious. It's structural.

Closed accounts disappear. Once an account closes, it moves from active systems to archive. The customer record becomes historical data. In many institutions, closed accounts are purged entirely after seven years for storage efficiency. The ability to connect a closed account to a newly opened account at another institution simply doesn't exist.

Death is categorized as natural. When analysts build retention models, they typically exclude death-related closures as "natural attrition" unavoidable departures that don't reflect service quality or competitive positioning. This categorization made sense when death was a relatively rare event in any given year. It doesn't make sense when death is becoming the dominant reason customers leave.

Beneficiaries are new customers. When a beneficiary inherits assets and opens an account, they appear in the system as a new customer, not as a retained relationship. The system has no way to connect the new account to the deceased's original account. From a data perspective, the inheritance never happened, there was simply an account closure and an unrelated account opening (if the beneficiary stays) or an account closure and nothing (if they don't).

Cross-generational data is siloed. Even when beneficiaries maintain accounts at the same institution, the relationship between their accounts and the deceased's accounts is rarely captured. The data that would allow analysis, "this customer inherited from that customer" doesn't exist in structured form.

No one owns the metric. Retention is typically owned by marketing or customer experience teams. Death processing is owned by operations or compliance. These teams don't talk to each other. The question "what happens to inherited deposits?" falls between organizational boundaries and gets asked by no one.

The result is systematic blindness. You can't manage what you don't measure, and you can't measure what you don't define. "Beneficiary retention" isn't a metric because it isn't a concept that exists in most institutions' analytical vocabulary.

The Hidden Hemorrhage

Let me show you what this blindness costs.

Take a mid-sized community bank with $3 billion in deposits and 50,000 deposit customers. Assume the customer base mirrors national demographics, roughly 15% are age 75 or older, the cohort most likely to die in any given year.

That's 7,500 customers in the peak mortality cohort.

If we assume an annual mortality rate of 8% for this age group (a reasonable estimate), approximately 600 of these customers will die each year.

If the average account balance for this cohort is $80,000 (older customers tend to have higher balances), that represents $48 million in deposits that will transfer to beneficiaries each year.

Now apply the industry retention statistics:

- If 80% of beneficiaries change institutions at inheritance, the bank loses $38.4 million annually.
- If even 50% of beneficiaries leave, the bank loses $24 million annually.
- Over a decade, that's $240 million to $384 million in lost deposits, from this single customer cohort alone.

And this is a conservative estimate. It doesn't include customers age 65-74 (a large and growing cohort). It doesn't include younger customers who die unexpectedly. It doesn't account for the cascade effect of family departures. It doesn't factor in the accelerating pace of Boomer mortality as the generation ages.

The actual number is almost certainly higher. But even the conservative estimate should be alarming: a mid-sized bank losing 1-2% of deposits annually to beneficiary attrition, with no awareness that it's happening.

Where does this appear in the bank's metrics?

Nowhere.

The retention rate remains 95%. The customer satisfaction scores remain high. The board presentations remain optimistic. The hemorrhage continues.

The Competitor's Gift

While traditional banks ignore beneficiary retention, others haven't noticed the opportunity.

Digital banks and neobanks have built their entire customer acquisition strategy around friction. They know that customers don't switch banks for fun, they switch when something forces them to act. Death is the ultimate forcing function. A beneficiary who must deal with a complex estate at one institution and a seamless digital experience at another will draw conclusions about where they want to bank.

Wealth management platforms are expanding into banking services specifically to capture wealth transfer flows. They understand that controlling the inheritance experience means controlling the next generation's financial relationship. If they can make estate settlement easier, they capture not just investment assets but deposits, lending relationships, and the entire household.

Fintech estate services are emerging to fill the gap that traditional banks have left open. Companies that specialize in estate settlement, beneficiary services, and wealth transfer are positioning themselves as intermediaries between deceased customers and their heirs. They may not be banks themselves, but they're capturing the relationship, and they're happy to refer heirs to whichever institution offers the best partnership terms.

Every one of these competitors is measuring what traditional banks aren't. They track conversion rates, time-to-resolution, beneficiary satisfaction, and asset capture. They treat estate settlement as a customer acquisition channel, not an operational burden. They're building the data infrastructure that traditional banks lack.

And they're growing.

The Spousal Transfer Trap

Before inherited assets reach the next generation, they often pass through an intermediate step: the surviving spouse.

This creates what I call the "spousal transfer trap" a double jeopardy that many institutions fail to recognize.

First transfer: From deceased spouse to surviving spouse.

When a husband dies, his assets typically transfer to his wife (or vice versa). In community property states, this transfer may be automatic for joint assets. In other states, it may require probate. Either way, the surviving spouse now controls assets that were previously jointly managed.

Research shows that 70% of widows switch their primary financial institution within a year of their husband's death. The reasons are numerous: feeling ignored by advisors who spoke mainly to the husband, receiving condescending treatment when asking questions, experiencing frustrating estate settlement processes, or simply wanting a fresh start unburdened by painful associations.

Whatever the reason, the institution that held the couple's accounts for decades loses the surviving spouse's business almost immediately.

Second transfer: From surviving spouse to children.

The surviving spouse typically lives another 5-15 years (women outlive men by an average of five years, and spouses are often younger than the deceased). When they die, the assets transfer again, this time to the children or other heirs.

If the surviving spouse stayed at the original institution, the children now face the same retention challenge. But if the surviving spouse left, the original institution has no relationship with the children at all. The assets have already moved once; they're not coming back.

The compound loss:

Consider a scenario: A husband dies at age 82 with $1 million at First Community Bank. His wife, age 78, inherits the funds. Within nine months, frustrated by the estate settlement process and feeling underserved, she moves the assets to a digital wealth manager that her daughter recommended.

The wife lives another ten years. She passed at age 88 with $1.2 million (the assets appreciated). Her daughter inherits.

But the daughter's inheritance never touches First Community Bank. The relationship was broken in the first transfer. The original institution doesn't just lose the deceased husband's deposits, they lose the wife's deposits, the daughter's inheritance, and any chance of serving the daughter's household.

One death. Two transfers. Permanent relationship loss.

What Good Measurement Looks Like

If you wanted to actually understand beneficiary retention at your institution, what would you need to measure?

Pre-death data:

- Total deposits held by customers who die each quarter/year
- Average balance by age cohort
- Account structure (joint vs. individual, POD vs. non-POD)
- Relationship depth (multiple account types, loans, other products)

- Family relationships captured in system (beneficiaries, authorized signers, joint holders)

Estate processing data:

- Time from death notification to beneficiary contact
- Time from death notification to Letters Testamentary receipt (if applicable)
- Time from Letters Testamentary to beneficiary account access
- Number of customer contacts required
- Number of branch visits required
- Customer effort score for estate processing

Post-death data:

- Percentage of beneficiaries who open accounts at the institution
- Percentage of inherited deposits retained at 30/90/180/365 days
- Beneficiary satisfaction scores
- Net Promoter Score (a standard measure of customer loyalty and satisfaction) for estate experience
- Destination of departed deposits (if trackable)

Long-term data:

- Beneficiary relationship expansion over 3-5 years
- Beneficiary referral rates
- Beneficiary lifetime value comparison to general population

Most institutions can answer zero of these questions with current data infrastructure. They may be able to partially answer one or two with significant manual effort. But none of this is tracked systematically, reported regularly, or used for management decision-making.

The first step toward solving the retention problem is admitting you don't know how bad it is.

The False Comfort of "Not Our Problem"

When I present these statistics to banking executives, I sometimes hear a response that goes something like this: "Those numbers are from wealth management. Our customers are different. They're more loyal. They have local ties. They won't leave just because the estate process is difficult."

This is wishful thinking.

The wealth management statistics may actually understate the problem for traditional banks. Here's why:

Wealth managers actively court heirs. An investment advisor who knows a client is aging will often meet with the client's adult children, explain services, and begin building a relationship. They're trying to prevent attrition because they know it's coming. Banks do almost none of this proactive relationship-building.

Wealth managers offer more personalized service. High-net-worth clients expect and receive concierge-level attention during estate settlement. They have a named advisor who guides them through the process. Bank customers get call centers and branch employees who may never have processed a death claim before.

Wealth managers compete on relationship. The value proposition of a wealth manager is expertise and personal attention. The value proposition of a bank is often.. lower fees? Convenience? These are easily replicated by competitors, especially digital ones.

If anything, beneficiaries may be more likely to leave a bank than a wealth manager, because the switching costs are lower and the relationship was always more transactional.

The assumption that many community banks and regional institutions make, that local ties and personal relationships will keep beneficiaries loyal, is particularly dangerous. Yes, the 82-year-old customer who banked with you for 40 years felt loyalty. But her 55-year-old daughter lives two states away and has never set foot in your branch. Her 58-year-old son lives locally but banks with a national institution. Your relationship was with the deceased, not with the heirs.

Loyalty doesn't transfer. Trust must be earned with each generation.

The Measurement Imperative

If you aren't uncomfortable right now, you haven't been paying attention.

You should be wondering: How much are we actually losing? You should be asking: Why don't we know this? You should be concerned that your strategic planning is based on a retention rate that excludes the most consequential customer departures your institution will ever experience.

That discomfort is appropriate. It's the first step toward action.

In the coming chapters, we'll examine why estate processing fails (Chapter 4), how operations compound the problem (Chapter 5), and how technology debt prevents solutions (Chapter 6). We'll explore the competitive opportunity (Chapters 7-9) and provide frameworks for action (Chapters 10-12).

But none of that matters if you don't start measuring.

Here is what I would ask you to do before you finish this book: Before you finish this book, commission a study of beneficiary retention at your institution. It doesn't need to be perfect. It doesn't need to capture every variable. It just needs to answer the basic question: When a customer dies, what percentage of their deposits remain at our institution one year later?

The answer will almost certainly be worse than you expect. And that answer is the beginning of transformation.

You can't manage what you don't measure. You can't fix what you won't acknowledge. And you can't win the Great Wealth Transfer by pretending it isn't happening.

The retention rate you report to your board is an illusion. The real number, the one that determines your institution's future, is hiding in plain sight, waiting for someone to find it.

CHAPTER FOUR

The Regulatory Maze

If you want to understand why death claims take so long to process, you need to understand the regulatory environment in which financial institutions operate. Banks aren't deliberately unhelpful, despite what frustrated beneficiaries often assume. Nor is it, as some executives believe, that their processes are simply "conservative by nature."

The truth is both more complex and more forgivable: the American financial system was never designed to transfer wealth at scale. What exists today isn't a system at all, it's an accumulation of fifty state probate regimes, overlapping federal compliance requirements, and institutional risk frameworks that evolved independently over decades. The result is a maze so intricate that even experienced estate attorneys sometimes get lost.

This chapter won't make you a regulatory expert. But it will give you the vocabulary to understand why your institution operates the way it does, and where the opportunities for improvement actually lie.

Fifty States, Fifty Systems

The United States has no federal probate law.

This single fact explains more about the friction in estate processing than any other. When a customer dies, the rules that govern how their assets transfer depend entirely on where they lived, where they owned property, and, in some cases, where their beneficiaries reside.

Each state has developed its own probate code, its own court procedures, its own documentary requirements, and its own timeline. The variations aren't minor.

Small estate thresholds range from $10,000 in some states to over $200,000 in others. In California, as of April 2025, estates with personal property valued under $208,850 can use a simplified Small Estate Affidavit process. In New York, the threshold for a "voluntary administration" is $50,000. In Texas, the small estate affidavit applies to estates under $75,000. A beneficiary inheriting a $100,000 account faces dramatically different processes depending solely on which state's laws apply.

Creditor claim periods vary from four months to a full year. During this period, the estate typically can't make final distributions. A family waiting to receive an inheritance has no control over this timeline, it's set by statute.

Executor authority differs by state. In some jurisdictions, an executor named in a will can begin acting immediately upon death, with court confirmation following later. In others, the executor has no authority whatsoever until the court issues Letters Testamentary. A bank that releases funds to an executor before the court has granted authority could face liability, even if the executor is legitimately named in a valid will.

Property classification adds another layer. Nine states, Arizona, California, Idaho, Louisiana, Nevada, New Mexico, Texas, Washington, and Wisconsin, follow community property rules, where assets acquired during marriage are presumed to be owned equally by both spouses. The remaining 41 states follow common law property rules, with different presumptions about ownership. When a married customer dies, determining who owns what depends on which system applies, and that determination affects everything from spousal rights to tax treatment.

For a financial institution operating across multiple states, this patchwork creates genuine operational challenges. A single policy can't accommodate fifty different legal frameworks. Documentation requirements that are sufficient in one state may be inadequate in another. Timelines that seem excessive to a beneficiary in California may actually be compressed compared to what the law requires in New York.

The KYC Problem

When a bank opens an account, it's required by federal law to verify the customer's identity. This process, known as Know Your Customer (commonly called KYC in the industry), is a cornerstone of anti-money laundering (AML) compliance, a set of procedures required under the Bank Secrecy Act to prevent illicit funds from moving through the financial system.

The original customer went through this process. The bank verified their name, date of birth, address, and Social Security number. It screened them against sanctions lists and watchlists. It assessed their risk profile. Over time, it built a transactional history that became part of the customer's ongoing monitoring.

When that customer dies, everything resets.

The beneficiary, even if they're the customer's child or spouse, is a new person to the bank's compliance systems. They must be verified from scratch. Their identity must be confirmed. They must be screened against the same sanctions lists and watchlists. If they're taking control of funds, they're effectively becoming a new customer for compliance purposes.

This isn't bureaucratic obstinacy. It's federal law.

The USA PATRIOT Act, passed in 2001, expanded AML requirements significantly and imposed Customer Identification Program (CIP) obligations, which require banks to verify the identity of every person who opens an account, on financial institutions. FinCEN (the Financial Crimes Enforcement Network, a bureau within the U.S. Treasury) issues regulations and guidance that banks must follow. The consequences of failure are severe: in recent years, financial institutions have paid billions of dollars in penalties for AML deficiencies.

Consider the bank's position: A person walks into a branch claiming to be the executor of an estate. They have a death certificate and a document they say is a will. They want access to an account containing hundreds of thousands of dollars.

From the bank's compliance perspective, the questions are immediate and serious:

- Is the death certificate genuine?
- Is the will valid and hasn't been superseded?
- Is this person actually the executor named in the will?
- Has the probate court authorized this person to act?

- Are there other claimants to the estate?
- Will releasing funds facilitate fraud or money laundering?

The answer is: the bank doesn't know any of these things without documentation. And the documentation required to establish confidence, Letters Testamentary from a court, verified identification, sometimes court orders for specific transactions, takes time to obtain.

The Fraud Landscape

Banks aren't paranoid about estate fraud because they enjoy being suspicious. They're paranoid because estate fraud is real, common, and expensive.

Consider the vulnerabilities:

Forged documents. Death certificates can be counterfeited. Wills can be fabricated. Letters Testamentary can be altered. Court stamps can be faked. Every document in the estate process is a potential point of fraud.

Identity theft. The deceased's identity is valuable precisely because it's no longer being monitored. The Social Security Administration's Death Master File, intended to prevent fraud, often takes months to update. During that window, fraudsters can open accounts, apply for credit, and redirect assets using the deceased's information.

Family disputes. Not all fraud comes from strangers. Family members sometimes present forged documents, conceal assets, or misrepresent their authority. Banks have been sued by legitimate heirs for releasing funds to fraudulent claimants, and by claimants for refusing to release funds to legitimate heirs. Both outcomes carry liability.

Elder financial exploitation. In some cases, the fraud began before death. A caregiver, family member, or other person may have obtained powers of attorney or beneficiary designations through undue influence. After death, these arrangements may appear legitimate on paper but may have been obtained through exploitation.

The scale of the problem is difficult to quantify because much of it goes unreported. But industry estimates suggest that estate and inheritance fraud costs billions annually. Financial institutions that release funds improperly, even in good faith, can be held liable for the losses.

This creates an institutional bias toward caution. From the bank's perspective, the cost of a wrongful release (potential lawsuit, regulatory scrutiny, reputation damage) is far higher than the cost of delay (customer frustration, complaint calls, occasional lost business). The incentives are misaligned with customer experience.

The Documentation Stack

When you understand the regulatory context, the documentation requirements start to make sense, even if they remain frustrating.

A typical estate claim requires:

Death Certificate. This is the foundational document, but it's not as simple as it sounds. Banks typically require certified copies (not photocopies). Some transactions require multiple certified copies because each institution keeps one for its files. Depending on the state and county, obtaining certified copies can take days to weeks. During the pandemic, some vital records offices faced backlogs of months.

Letters Testamentary (or Letters of Administration). This court-issued document is the only proof that someone has legal authority to act on behalf of an estate. A will, by itself, isn't sufficient, the will must be probated, and the executor must be formally appointed. In intestate cases (no will), the court appoints an administrator and issues Letters of Administration instead. Either document typically requires a court filing, a hearing, and processing time.

Executor Identification. The bank must verify that the person presenting the Letters Testamentary is actually the person named in those letters. This typically requires government-issued photo identification. If the executor lives in a different state than the deceased, additional verification may be required.

Estate Tax Identification Number (EIN). Before the estate can conduct business, including opening an estate account to hold and manage assets, it needs its own tax identification number, separate from the deceased's

Social Security number. Fortunately, EINs can be obtained quickly through the IRS, often online and in minutes.

Account-Specific Documentation. Depending on the transaction, additional documents may be required. Accessing a safe deposit box may require a court order in some states. Liquidating investment accounts may require separate forms from the investment subsidiary. Transferring real property may require deed filings with the county. Each asset class has its own process.

Affidavits and Letters of Instruction. For transfers above certain thresholds, or for specific actions like wire transfers, banks typically require notarized documents specifying exactly what the executor wants done. This creates an audit trail and protects the bank from claims that it acted without proper authorization.

The aggregate effect is what beneficiaries experience as an endless paper chase. Each document has a purpose, but the purposes aren't always explained, and the documents aren't always requested at once. A family might make multiple trips to the branch, each time discovering another requirement they hadn't anticipated.

The Liability Calculus

Financial institutions are fiduciaries in a specific sense: they hold other people's money and must exercise care in releasing it. This fiduciary role creates liability exposure that shapes every policy decision.

Wrongful release. If a bank releases funds to someone who isn't entitled to them, whether due to fraud, mistake, or inadequate verification, the bank can be liable to the rightful heirs for the full amount plus damages. Courts have held banks liable even when they relied on apparently valid documents, if they failed to exercise reasonable care.

Wrongful refusal. Conversely, if a bank refuses to release funds to someone who's legitimately entitled to them, the bank can be liable for damages caused by the delay. These cases are less common, partly because the damages are harder to quantify, but they do occur, particularly when banks maintain unreasonable documentation requirements or ignore valid court orders.

Fiduciary liability to the estate. In some cases, banks serve as trustees or executors of estates. In this capacity, they owe fiduciary duties to the beneficiaries and can be personally liable for mismanagement. Even banks that don't serve in formal fiduciary roles may face claims that they aided or enabled a breach of fiduciary duty by an executor.

Regulatory liability. Beyond private lawsuits, banks face regulatory scrutiny for their estate-handling practices. Examiners from the FDIC, OCC, NCUA, or state banking departments may review policies and procedures as part of routine examinations. Deficiencies in documentation, verification, or record-keeping can result in formal enforcement actions.

This liability landscape explains why banks err on the side of caution. The downside of being too slow is customer frustration. The downside of being too fast is lawsuits and regulatory action. Given these asymmetric risks, conservative processing is the rational institutional choice, even if it's not the optimal customer experience. However this can be adjusted to improve the customer experience.

The FDIC Grace Period

There's one area where federal regulation actually helps beneficiaries, though few people know about it.

The FDIC insures deposits up to $250,000 per depositor, per institution, per ownership category. Different ownership categories, individual accounts, joint accounts, trust accounts, are insured separately. This can allow a single depositor to have coverage well in excess of $250,000 at one bank if their accounts are properly structured.

What happens when a depositor dies? The ownership structure of their accounts may change. A joint account becomes a single-owner account. A trust account's beneficiaries may change. These shifts could theoretically affect insurance coverage.

To address this, the FDIC provides a six-month "grace period" after a depositor's death. During this period, insurance coverage continues as if the depositor were still alive, giving the estate time to restructure accounts without risking loss of coverage. This is one of the few regulatory provisions explicitly designed to ease estate transitions.

The NCUA provides a similar grace period for credit union accounts. For six months after a member's death, the credit union will insure their accounts as if they were still alive.

These grace periods are helpful but remarkably little-known. Most beneficiaries have never heard of them. More concerning, many frontline bank employees are unaware they exist either, which means families often receive incomplete guidance during the most critical window of the estate process.

State Banking Department Variations

Beyond federal regulation, each state has its own banking department with its own examination procedures, consumer protection rules, and enforcement priorities.

Some state banking departments have issued specific guidance on deceased account processing. Others have consumer complaint processes that can pressure banks to resolve estate disputes. A few have statutory provisions governing how quickly banks must process certain estate claims.

But there's no uniformity. What passes the examination in one state may draw criticism in another. What's required by regulation in California may be discretionary in Texas. Banks operating across multiple states face the challenge of reconciling these varying expectations into coherent national policies, a reconciliation that often defaults to the most conservative requirements across all jurisdictions.

What Regulation Doesn't Require

Here's what's important for bank executives to understand: most of the delay in estate processing isn't mandated by regulation.

Regulation requires:

- Verification of identity and authority
- Compliance with AML/KYC requirements
- Adherence to state probate procedures
- Reasonable care in releasing funds

Regulation doesn't require:

- Three-week appointments for estate services
- Seven-to-ten-day internal processing queues
- Multiple branch visits for sequential document collection
- Separate processes for each account type
- Manual review of every document by multiple departments

The gap between what regulation requires and what banks actually do is where the opportunity lies. Understanding this gap is critical, because much of what families experience as bureaucratic obstruction is actually internal policy layered on top of regulatory minimums.

Most banks have built estate processing systems that far exceed regulatory minimums, not because regulators demanded it, but because internal risk management, legacy technology, siloed departments, and institutional inertia have accumulated over decades. These systems were designed for a world where estate claims were rare exceptions. They weren't designed for a world where death is the most common reason customers leave.

Understanding this distinction is essential. When a bank executive says "we can't do that because of compliance," the question to ask is: ***Is that actually a regulatory requirement, or is it a policy we've created that we've come to believe is required?***

In most cases, it's the latter.

The Path Through the Maze

Regulation isn't the enemy of good customer experience. It's a constraint, a real one, but constraints can be managed.

Consider what excellent estate processing would look like, even within current regulatory requirements:

Single point of contact. Instead of bouncing beneficiaries between branches, call centers, and specialist departments, assign a dedicated estate specialist who shepherds each case from notification to resolution. This changes nothing about compliance requirements; it changes everything about customer experience.

Document collection at intake. Instead of discovering documentation requirements one at a time over multiple visits, provide beneficiaries with a complete checklist at first contact, customized for their state and situation.

Better yet, help them understand which documents they'll need before they even have them, so they can plan accordingly.

Parallel processing. Instead of sequential queues (branch review, then estate services review, then legal review, then operations), process documents through multiple departments simultaneously. Compliance requirements don't mandate sequential processing; that's an operational choice.

Proactive communication. Instead of waiting for beneficiaries to call and ask for updates, reach out proactively with status information. Automation can handle most of this. A simple text message saying "your documents have been received and are under review" costs almost nothing and transforms the experience.

Empathy training. Instead of scripted responses that feel cold and bureaucratic, train staff to acknowledge grief, express genuine condolences, and communicate with warmth even while enforcing necessary requirements. Compliance doesn't prohibit kindness.

None of these improvements require regulatory change. They require institutional will.

The Regulatory Future

There are signs that regulators are becoming more attentive to estate processing issues, though change is slow.

The Consumer Financial Protection Bureau (CFPB) has received increasing complaints about estate handling and has included questions about deceased account management in some examination processes. State attorneys general have pursued cases against financial institutions for egregious estate-handling failures. Industry groups like the American Bankers Association have published best practices guides (though compliance is voluntary).

More significant change may come from market pressure rather than regulatory mandate. As the Great Wealth Transfer accelerates, institutions that handle death well will capture enormous asset flows. Those that handle it poorly will lose not just the deceased's accounts but the entire family's business, often permanently.

The smartest regulators understand this. A financial system that systematically fails families during their most vulnerable moments isn't a stable financial system. At some point, regulatory attention will follow public frustration.

Whether your institution leads that change or is forced into it is a strategic choice.

The Key Insight

The core insight from this chapter is straightforward:

Regulation is real but not determinative. Yes, compliance requirements constrain what banks can do. Yes, state-by-state variation creates genuine complexity. Yes, liability concerns justify caution. But within these constraints, enormous latitude exists for better design.

Most delay is policy, not law. When processing takes months, the driver is usually internal systems, staffing levels, technology limitations, and accumulated procedure, not regulatory mandate. These are things institutions can change.

Regulators follow markets. If your institution creates a genuinely better estate experience, regulators are unlikely to object. They may eventually require others to match it. Being conservative isn't the same as being compliant; it's a choice masquerading as a constraint.

The maze is navigable. Families navigate this maze every day, usually without guidance. Institutions that serve as guides, helping families understand what's required and why, anticipating their needs, and smoothing the path, will earn loyalty that lasts generations.

The regulatory environment is complex. But complexity isn't an excuse. It's a competitive advantage for those willing to master it.

CHAPTER FIVE

The Operational Tangle

In Chapter 4, we explored the regulatory constraints that shape estate processing, the maze of state probate laws, KYC requirements, and compliance obligations that make even simple estates complex. Those constraints are real, but they account for perhaps 20% of processing time.

This chapter is about the other 80%. And this is the part that's entirely in your hands.

The operational tangle is the accumulation of internal processes, departmental handoffs, system limitations, and institutional habits that transform a two-week regulatory requirement into a six-month ordeal. It's the difference between what the law requires and what your institution actually does. It's the gap between policy intent and operational reality.

Understanding this tangle is essential because, unlike regulation, it's entirely within your control.

The Anatomy of a Handoff

Let me walk you through what happens inside a typical institution when a death notification arrives.

Day 1: Branch Intake

A family member walks into a branch to report that their mother has died. The branch employee, let's call her Janie, has processed perhaps three death notifications in her five-year career. She's sympathetic but uncertain about the procedure.

Janie knows she needs to document the notification, but she's not sure which form to use. She checks with her branch manager, who directs her to a rarely-accessed section of the policy manual. She finds the form, fills it out with the family member's information, and collects a copy of the death certificate.

Now what?

Janie needs to notify the estate services department, but she's not entirely sure how. She sends an email to an address she finds in the policy manual. She also puts the physical documents in the branch's outgoing mail to the operations center, because that's what she was taught to do with important documents.

Time elapsed: 45 minutes of the family member's time. Janie's confidence: moderate. Probability that the email and physical mail will arrive at the same place: uncertain.

Days 2 - 5: Routing

The email arrives in a shared inbox monitored by the estate services team. The inbox receives approximately 200 emails per day on various topics. Estate-related emails are flagged and sorted by a rotating team member. Janie's email is categorized as a "death notification, initial" and added to a queue.

Meanwhile, the physical documents arrive at the operations center, where they're scanned, categorized, and uploaded to a document management system. The scanning team doesn't know that an email has already been sent about this case; they process the documents according to standard procedure.

By Day 5, the estate services team has received both the email notification and the scanned documents, but in different systems. Someone needs to connect them.

Days 6 - 10: Case Creation

A case manager in estate services, let's call him David, picks up Janie's email from the queue. He opens the core banking system to look up the deceased customer's accounts. He finds a checking account, a savings account, two CDs, and a safe deposit box.

David creates a case file in the case management system, documenting the accounts and the notification date. He then needs to locate the scanned documents to attach to the case. This requires searching the document management system by name and date range, because the scanning system assigned its own reference number that doesn't match David's case number.

David finds the documents, downloads them, and uploads them to the case management system. He reviews them: a death certificate and a note from Janie, but no Letters Testamentary as required by the state they're in. The case can't proceed until court documentation is received.

David sends a letter to the family member, using a template from the correspondence system, explaining what additional documentation is required. The letter goes into the outgoing mail queue. It will be printed and mailed tomorrow.

Days 11 - 15: Waiting

The family receives David's letter on Day 13. They don't have Letters Testamentary yet because they've only just filed for probate. They put the letter aside, planning to respond when they have the documents.

David's case sits in a "pending documentation" status. No action is required until the family submits additional documents. The case management system will send an automated reminder in 30 days if no documents are received.

Days 45 - 50: Documentation Received

Six weeks later, the family obtained Letters Testamentary. They mail the documents to the address on David's letter, which is the estate services correspondence address, not the scanning center address.

The documents arrive at estate services, where they sit in a physical inbox until someone processes the incoming mail. They're eventually scanned and uploaded, but now there's a new matching challenge: connecting these documents to David's existing case.

David is on vacation this week. His cases have been reassigned to a colleague, Jennifer, who's covering for three other people. Jennifer locates the case, reviews the new documents, and determines that the Letters Testamentary are valid. She updates the case status to "documentation complete."

Days 51 - 60: Account Review

Now that documentation is complete, the case moves to the "account review" queue. A different team handles this step, the account operations team, which manages account freezes, balance transfers, and closures.

The account operations team receives a daily report of cases ready for review. They work through the queue in the order received. Jennifer's update appeared on Day 51; by Day 57, an account operations specialist named Robert reviews the case.

Robert logs into the core banking system and reviews each account. He needs to determine: Are there any holds or restrictions? Are there any automatic payments that need to be stopped? Are there any linked accounts at other institutions? Is there a safe deposit box, and if so, what's the procedure?

Robert discovers that the checking account has an automatic payment to a utility company and another to a credit card. He freezes the automatic payments. He also notes the safe deposit box and flags the case for the branch, safe deposit access requires an in-person appointment with a branch manager.

Robert updates the case and moves it to "ready for distribution" status, but first, the CDs need to be addressed. Early withdrawal of CDs requires approval from a supervisor. Robert sends the case to his supervisor, Lynn for approval.

Days 61 - 65: Approval and Coordination

Lynn reviews the CD situation. One CD has a maturity date in three months; the other matures in eight months. She approves early withdrawal of both, noting the penalty amounts in the file.

The case is now ready for distribution, except for the safe deposit box. The branch needs to schedule an appointment with the executor to access the box. Robert sends a notification to the branch through the internal messaging system.

The branch manager receives the notification but doesn't recognize the customer name. She looks up the customer in the system and sees that they banked at a different branch across town. She forwards the notification to the correct branch.

Days 66 - 75: Safe Deposit Box Coordination

The correct branch receives the notification. The branch manager, Thomas, calls the executor to schedule an appointment. The executor is available next Tuesday, eight days from now.

On Tuesday, the executor arrives at the branch. Thomas opens the safe deposit box in the presence of the executor and a witness, as required by state law. The contents are inventoried and released to the executor. Thomas updates the case file to indicate that the safe deposit box has been cleared.

Days 76 - 80: Distribution

With all components addressed, accounts reviewed, CDs liquidated (with penalties calculated), and safe deposit box cleared, the case is finally ready for distribution.

But wait: the executor needs to open an estate account to receive the funds. This requires another branch visit. And before the estate account can be opened, the executor needs an EIN from the IRS, which they may or may not have obtained.

The executor calls to ask about next steps. They're connected to the general customer service line, where a representative looks up the case and provides information, but the representative doesn't have access to the full case file, only to the account information visible in the customer-facing system. They direct the executor to visit a branch.

The executor visits a branch, a different branch than the one with the safe deposit box, and asks to open an estate account. The branch employee looks up the case, confirms the documentation is complete, and opens the account. This takes approximately 45 minutes.

Now the executor can request a transfer of funds from the deceased's accounts to the estate account.

Days 81 - 90: Transfer and Closure

The executor submits a written request for the transfer. This request goes to the account operations team for processing. Transfers over a certain threshold require a supervisor's approval. The transfer is approved on Day 85.

The deceased's accounts are closed. The case status is updated to "complete." Total elapsed time: approximately 90 days.

The Handoff Inventory

Count the handoffs in that story:

1. Family member to branch employee (Janie)
2. Branch employee to estate services (via email and physical mail)
3. Physical documents to scanning center
4. Scanning center to document management system
5. Email notification to case manager (David)
6. Case manager to document management system (manual retrieval)
7. Case manager to correspondence system (letter generation)
8. Case manager to family (via mail)
9. Family to estate services (documentation return)
10. Incoming mail to case file (manual matching)
11. Original case manager to covering case manager (Jennifer)
12. Estate services to account operations (Robert)
13. Account operations to supervisor (Lynn)
14. Estate services to branch (safe deposit notification)
15. Wrong branch to correct branch (forwarding)
16. Branch to executor (appointment scheduling)
17. Executor to customer service (phone inquiry)
18. Customer service to branch (redirect)
19. Branch to account operations (estate account opening)
20. Executor to account operations (transfer request)
21. Account operations to supervisor (transfer approval)

Twenty-one handoffs for a straightforward estate with no complications, no disputes, and cooperative beneficiaries.

Every handoff is an opportunity for delay. Every handoff is an opportunity for error. Every handoff is a point where information can be lost, context can be stripped, and the human being at the center of this process, the grieving family member, can be forgotten.

The Departmental Reality

The handoff problem is a symptom of a deeper issue: departmental silos.

In most financial institutions, the functions required for estate processing are scattered across multiple departments:

Retail Banking / Branch Operations: Handles the initial notification, document collection, and customer-facing interactions. Branch employees may process death notifications so rarely that they never develop expertise or confidence.

Estate Services / Specialized Servicing: Manages the case, tracks documentation, and coordinates with other departments. This team may be centralized, serving multiple regions or the entire institution from a single location.

Account Operations: Executes account-level changes, freezes, transfers, closures, CD liquidations. This team often handles a wide variety of transactions, of which estate-related work is a small subset.

Compliance / Risk: Reviews documentation to ensure regulatory requirements are met. May be consulted on complex cases involving multi-state probate, foreign beneficiaries, or unusually large estates.

Legal: Involved when disputes arise, documentation is ambiguous, or liability concerns surface.

Customer Service / Call Center: Handles incoming inquiries from family members who don't know whom else to contact.

Each department has its own priorities, its own queue, its own systems, and its own metrics. Estate processing is rarely anyone's primary focus. It's exception handling, the work that arrives unexpectedly and disrupts the normal flow.

Research confirms the cost of this fragmentation. The Boston Consulting Group's 2019 analysis of large enterprises found that in siloed organizations, as much as 15% of total workforce capacity is consumed by redundant activities that exist solely because information and processes don't flow effectively across departmental boundaries. For a bank with 1,000 employees, that's 150 full-time equivalents dedicated to managing friction between departments, friction that customers experience as delay.

The Branch Problem

Nowhere is the operational tangle more acute than at the branch level.

Branch employees are generalists. They handle account openings, loan inquiries, teller transactions, and a hundred other tasks. Death notifications are rare, a typical branch might see one or two per month, which means individual employees may go many months between encounters.

When a death notification arrives, the branch employee faces immediate challenges:

Procedural uncertainty. Where is the policy? Which form do I use? Who do I contact? These questions require navigation of internal systems that the employee rarely accesses.

Emotional complexity. The person across the desk is grieving. They may be confused, upset, or frustrated. The employee must balance empathy with procedure, a difficult combination when they're uncertain of the procedure.

Time pressure. Other customers are waiting. The branch manager is watching productivity metrics. There's pressure to process the interaction quickly, but estate notifications require time and care.

Documentation anxiety. Is this death certificate valid? Are these Letters Testamentary current? What if I accept the wrong documents and create liability for the bank?

The result is often defensive processing: employees follow the most conservative interpretation of policy, require more documentation than necessary, and push decisions to specialists elsewhere in the organization. This protects the employee but creates delays for the family.

As one national bank executive described the historical situation: "Banking staff at branches typically dealt with only one bereavement a month, which meant they didn't always have the specialist knowledge to manage the client's financial estate. That could lead to mistakes such as sending the wrong amount to the wrong beneficiary, failing to obtain the correct documents, or miscalculating how to divide funds correctly when there were multiple beneficiaries."

The branch is the front door of estate processing, and it's often the most undertrained and underprepared point in the entire workflow.

The Technology Gap

Underlying the handoff problem and the departmental silos is a technology infrastructure that was never designed for estate processing.

Core banking systems manage accounts, balances, and transactions. They're optimized for individual account operations, not for workflows that span multiple accounts and multiple parties over extended timeframes.

Document management systems store scanned documents, but they're often disconnected from case management. Finding the right document for the right case requires manual searching and matching.

Case management systems track the status of complex processes, but they may not integrate smoothly with core banking or document management. Data must be manually transferred between systems.

Customer relationship management (CRM) systems capture customer information and interaction history, but they're typically focused on sales and service, not estate administration. The CRM may not recognize "the estate of [deceased customer]" as a valid entity.

Correspondence systems generate letters and notices, but they may use templates designed for live customers, requiring manual editing for estate communications.

The result is a patchwork of systems that don't talk to each other. Case managers toggle between five or six applications to do their jobs. Information entered in one system must be re-entered in another. Errors propagate because there's no single source of truth.

That same national bank estate services team found that before implementing workflow automation: "You would have to literally go to every department separately and report the person deceased for every product and service you own with us." Imagine being the family member who must make that journey, separate notifications for checking, savings, CDs, credit cards, loans, and safe deposit boxes.

The Measurement Void

What gets measured gets managed. Estate processing, for the most part, doesn't get measured.

Ask your operations team these questions:

- What is the average time from death notification to case closure?
- What percentage of cases are closed within 30/60/90/180 days?
- How many handoffs does the average case experience?
- What is the error rate in estate processing?
- How many customer contacts are required to close a typical case?
- What is the customer effort score for estate families?

In most institutions, these questions can't be answered. The data exists, scattered across case management systems, call logs, and branch records, but it has never been assembled into coherent metrics. Estate processing happens, but it happens invisibly.

Without metrics, improvement is impossible. You can't set targets if you don't know where you're starting. You can't identify bottlenecks if you can't see the workflow. You can't justify investment if you can't quantify the problem.

This measurement void is partly a technology problem, the systems don't produce the right reports, but it's mostly a priority problem. Nobody owns estate processing as a business function. It's distributed across departments, each of which measures its own activities but not the end-to-end journey.

The Cost Nobody Calculates

Estate processing consumes resources, but the cost is rarely calculated.

Consider the labor involved in that 90-day case we walked through:

- Branch employee (Janie): 45 minutes initial intake, plus occasional follow-up
- Case manager (David): 2 hours creating the case, locating documents, generating correspondence

- Covering case manager (Jennifer): 30 minutes reviewing returned documentation
- Account operations specialist (Robert): 1 hour reviewing accounts, coordinating branch notification
- Supervisor (Lynn): 15 minutes approving CD withdrawals
- Branch manager (Thomas): 1 hour safe deposit box access appointment
- Branch employee (estate account opening): 45 minutes
- Account operations (transfer processing): 30 minutes
- Supervisor (transfer approval): 15 minutes

Total: approximately 7-8 hours of staff time for a single, uncomplicated estate.

If your institution processes 500 estates per year, that's 3,500-4,000 hours of labor, roughly two full-time employees dedicated to estate processing, spread invisibly across departments.

But this calculation understates the true cost:

Rework and error correction. When documents are misfiled, when cases are misrouted, when beneficiaries receive incorrect information, someone must fix the problem. Error correction often takes more time than correct processing.

Escalations and complaints. When families become frustrated, they escalate. Escalations require supervisor involvement, research, and response. Severe complaints may require legal review. Each escalation consumes hours of staff time.

Opportunity cost. Every hour spent on estate processing is an hour not spent on revenue-generating activities. Branch employees processing death notifications aren't opening new accounts. Case managers handling estate paperwork aren't servicing active customers.

Retention cost. As we established in Chapter 3, poor estate processing drives beneficiaries away. The revenue lost from departing beneficiaries dwarfs the labor cost of processing, but because retention isn't tracked, the connection isn't made.

The total cost of estate processing, labor, errors, escalations, and lost relationships, probably exceeds the annual salary of a dedicated estate services team. But because the costs are scattered and invisible, the investment case is never made.

Exception Handling vs. Core Workflow

Here is the fundamental operational problem: estate processing is treated as exception handling when it should be treated as a core workflow.

Exception handling is what happens when something goes wrong, a transaction fails, a customer complains, a system errors. Exception handling is reactive, ad hoc, and inherently inefficient. It relies on escalation paths and supervisor intervention because there's no standardized process.

Core workflows, by contrast, are designed. They're documented, measured, and optimized. They have clear ownership, defined service-level agreements (SLAs), and continuous improvement cycles. They're staffed appropriately because their volume and complexity are understood.

Account opening is a core workflow. Loan origination is a core workflow. These processes have been analyzed, automated, and streamlined because they drive revenue and customer acquisition.

Estate processing isn't a core workflow. It's treated as a special case, something that happens when normal processing can't apply. It relies on the institutional knowledge of experienced staff, who are rarely asked to document their procedures or train their successors.

As long as estate processing remains exception handling, it will be underfunded, understaffed, and underperforming. The volume is there, your institution processes hundreds or thousands of estates per year. The complexity is there, regulatory requirements demand careful documentation and verification. The stakes are there, each estate represents a family in crisis and a relationship at risk.

What's missing is recognition that estate processing deserves the same operational attention as any other high-volume, high-stakes business process.

What Good Operations Look Like

Imagine a different model.

Single point of contact. When a death notification arrives, the family is assigned a dedicated estate specialist, not a case number, a person. This specialist guides them through the entire process, anticipates their needs, and proactively communicates status updates.

Centralized intake. Whether the notification arrives by branch, phone, mail, or online, it flows to a single team trained specifically in estate processing. The branch collects initial information, but case creation happens centrally by people who do this work every day.

Integrated systems. The estate specialist works in a single application that connects to core banking, document management, and correspondence. They can see all accounts, attach documents, generate letters, and update status without toggling between systems.

Parallel processing. Instead of sequential handoffs, multiple workstreams advance simultaneously. While the family gathers court documents, the institution inventories accounts and identifies potential issues. When documents arrive, the case is ready to proceed immediately.

Proactive communication. Status updates go out automatically: "We've received your documents and are reviewing." "Your case has been approved and is ready for distribution." "We've scheduled your appointment for Thursday." The family never wonders what's happening.

Measured and managed. Every case is tracked from notification to closure. Average cycle time, bottleneck identification, error rates, and satisfaction scores are reported weekly. Performance targets drive continuous improvement.

This isn't a fantasy. Some institutions, typically larger ones with dedicated estate services teams, have implemented versions of this model. Wells Fargo's Estate Care Centre, for example, used workflow automation to create case files automatically once the bank received confirmation that a customer had died, allowing staff to track status, coordinate across departments, and ensure that "the family never has to repeat their story."

The question isn't whether good operations are possible. The question is whether your institution will invest in building them.

The Staffing Equation

Let's return to our mid-sized community bank processing 500 estates per year.

If each estate requires 7-8 hours of labor (plus error correction and escalation), total annual labor is 4,000-5,000 hours, approximately two to two-and-a-half full-time employees.

That labor is currently scattered across 15-20 employees in multiple departments, none of whom specializes in estate processing. The result is inefficiency, inconsistency, and poor customer experience.

What if those 2-2.5 FTEs were consolidated into a dedicated estate services team?

Two full-time estate specialists could handle 500 estates per year, roughly one per business day each. They would develop expertise, build efficient processes, and deliver consistent quality.

A third position, part-time or shared, could handle supervision, training, and escalations. This person ensures quality control and serves as the point of contact for complex cases.

Branch employees would still handle initial intake, but with a clear handoff protocol. They would collect basic information and documents, then immediately transfer the case to the specialist team. No more uncertainty, no more policy-manual searches.

The total cost? Perhaps $180,000-$220,000 annually in fully-loaded compensation, depending on market and experience level.

The benefit? Dramatically improved processing times, reduced errors, better customer experience, and, most importantly, higher beneficiary retention. If the specialist team's work retains even 20-30 additional beneficiaries per year (at an average balance of $50,000), the revenue impact easily exceeds the cost.

This isn't a complex business case. It's simple math obscured by organizational fragmentation.

Breaking the Tangle

The operational tangle didn't form overnight, and it won't dissolve overnight. But every institution can take steps to begin unwinding it.

Step 1: Map the current process. Before you can improve estate processing, you need to understand it. Document every step, every handoff, every system touchpoint. Interview the people who do the work, branch employees, case managers, operations specialists. Ask them: What's hardest about this job? Where do things get stuck? What information do you wish you had?

Step 2: Measure what matters. Implement basic metrics: average time from notification to closure, number of customer contacts per case, error rate, escalation rate. Even rough metrics are better than none. What you measure, you can manage.

Step 3: Designate ownership. Someone, a person, not a committee, should own estate processing as a business function. This owner is responsible for end-to-end performance, cross-departmental coordination, and continuous improvement. They report on estate processing metrics alongside other operational metrics.

Step 4: Consolidate where possible. Look for opportunities to reduce handoffs. Can branch intake flow directly to a centralized team? Can document processing and case management be unified? Every eliminated handoff is reduced delay and reduced error risk.

Step 5: Invest in training. The people who handle estate notifications, especially branch employees, need better preparation. Develop training modules, quick-reference guides, and role-playing exercises. Make estate processing part of standard onboarding, not an afterthought discovered during the employee's first death notification.

Step 6: Fix the quick wins. Some improvements require no budget and minimal effort. Pre-populate documentation checklists so families know exactly what's required. Implement automatic status notifications. Create a single phone number that routes estate inquiries to the right team. These changes cost almost nothing and improve experience immediately.

Step 7: Build the business case for technology. If your systems don't support efficient estate processing, document the cost of manual workarounds. Quantify the hours lost to system-toggling, the errors caused by manual data entry, the delays caused by disconnected case management. This builds the justification for system investment.

None of these steps is revolutionary. Together, they transform estate processing from invisible exception handling to visible, manageable, improvable operations.

The Human Cost

Throughout this chapter, I've focused on operational mechanics: handoffs, systems, metrics, staffing. But underlying every process failure is a human cost.

Every week of delay is a week when a grieving family can't access the resources they need. Every miscommunication is a frustration added to an already overwhelming situation. Every error is a reminder that the institution doesn't understand or care about their circumstances.

The operational tangle isn't just inefficient. It's unkind.

Financial institutions often speak of their commitment to customer service, their dedication to community, their values of empathy and support. Those values are tested most severely in moments of loss, and tested most practically by the operations that serve families during those moments.

When your operations fail bereaved families, your values are just words.

When your operations serve bereaved families well, your values become tangible, visible, and memorable.

The operational tangle can be untangled. The handoffs can be reduced. The systems can be connected. The processes can be measured and improved.

The question is whether you will do the work.

CHAPTER SIX

The Technology Debt

In the previous two chapters, we examined the regulatory constraints and operational tangles that make estate processing difficult. Both are real challenges. But neither fully explains why improving estate processing feels so impossibly hard.

This chapter is about the technology underneath, the systems, the code, the architecture that shapes what's possible. It's about the choices made decades ago that still constrain what you can do today. It's about the hidden cost of not modernizing and the hidden risk of trying.

It's about technology debt, and why it may be the most consequential barrier between your institution and the future.

The Geological Reality

Imagine your institution's technology as geological strata. At the surface are the customer-facing applications, mobile banking, online portals, the interfaces that customers see and touch. These are relatively modern, relatively attractive, relatively responsive to change.

Dig deeper, and you find the middleware layer, the integration platforms, message queues, and service buses that connect systems together. This layer is less visible but essential, translating requests between systems that speak different languages.

Deeper still lies the core, the systems that actually hold the accounts, process transactions, maintain balances, and generate statements. These are the systems of record, the authoritative sources of truth about every customer, every account, every dollar.

And at the very bottom, in many institutions, lies something remarkable: code written in the 1960s and 1970s, still running, still processing billions of transactions, still holding the institution together.

This is the geological reality of banking technology. The surface changes frequently; the core changes almost never. And the deeper you go, the harder change becomes.

The COBOL Truth

Let me tell you about COBOL.

COBOL, which stands for Common Business-Oriented Language, was one of the earliest computer programming languages, created in 1959. It was designed for business data processing: payroll, accounting, banking transactions. It was built to be stable, reliable, and readable. And in those objectives, it succeeded spectacularly.

Today, COBOL remains foundational to global finance. Reuters reports that 43% of core banking systems in the United States are built on COBOL. Industry analysts estimate that 220 billion lines of COBOL code remain in operation worldwide, processing approximately $3 trillion in daily transactions. COBOL powers 95% of ATM transactions globally. It handles 80% of in-person transactions at financial institutions.

If COBOL stopped working tomorrow, the global financial system would collapse.

Here is the problem: the people who wrote this code are dying.

The average COBOL programmer is approximately 58-60 years old. Approximately 10% retire each year. By some estimates, there will be 84,000 or more unfilled mainframe positions over the coming years as this generation exits the workforce. Universities stopped teaching COBOL decades ago. Young developers have no interest in learning it. The talent pipeline isn't just shrinking, it's nearly empty.

As one Accenture executive put it bluntly: "It's not so much that an individual may have retired, he may have expired, so there's no option to get him or her to come back."

This creates an extraordinary vulnerability. The systems that process your customers' accounts, including the accounts of deceased customers, are maintained by a shrinking pool of aging specialists who are increasingly expensive and increasingly difficult to find. Some institutions pay COBOL engineers $200-250 per hour, two to three times the rate of developers working on modern technology stacks.

And even when you find someone who knows COBOL, they may not understand your institution's specific COBOL. Core banking systems have accumulated decades of customizations, workarounds, and patches. The business logic is embedded in millions of lines of code that were never properly documented. The original developers are long gone. In many cases, institutions are literally running code without fully understanding what it does or what might break if it's changed.

The 70% Problem

The COBOL challenge is just one manifestation of a broader reality: technology debt consumes the majority of most institutions' IT budgets.

Industry research consistently shows that banks spend 60 - 80% of their technology budgets simply maintaining existing systems. Some estimates are even higher, one analysis found that banks spend up to 70 cents of every IT dollar on legacy maintenance. Credit unions face an even more extreme version: approximately 90% of technology budgets devoted to keeping existing systems running, leaving only 10% for innovation.

Think about what this means. For every dollar your institution invests in technology, 60 - 70 cents or more goes to keeping yesterday's systems alive. Only 30 - 40 cents, at best, goes toward building anything new.

McKinsey research reinforces this picture: the consulting firm estimates that only 5 - 10 cents of every technology dollar actually delivers business value. The rest is consumed by maintenance, patching, integration overhead, and working around the limitations of legacy systems.

This is the 70% problem. The majority of your technology investment isn't building your future, it's maintaining your past. And the longer you wait to address it, the worse the ratio becomes. Technical debt compounds. Maintenance costs increase 10 - 15% annually after systems age past their warranty periods. The pool of people who can maintain old systems shrinks. The cost of not modernizing grows every year.

The Spaghetti Architecture

Legacy systems would be challenging enough if they existed in isolation. But they don't. Over decades, institutions have added system after system, each one connected to others through a web of integrations, interfaces, and data feeds.

The industry has a term for this: spaghetti architecture. It's the accumulation of point-to-point connections, custom interfaces, middleware layers, and integration workarounds that turn a technology landscape into an incomprehensible tangle.

In a spaghetti architecture, changing anything is dangerous. Every system depends on other systems in ways that may not be fully documented or understood. Upgrading one component can break connections to five others. Adding a new capability requires navigating a maze of existing integrations. What looks like a simple enhancement, say, adding a new field to customer records, can trigger a cascade of changes across dozens of systems.

Estate processing suffers particularly from spaghetti architecture because it must touch so many systems:

- Core banking for account information and balances
- Document management for death certificates and court documents
- Case management for tracking workflow status
- Customer relationship management for contact information and interaction history
- Correspondence systems for generating letters and notices
- Payment systems for processing transfers and distributions
- Safe deposit systems for box access coordination
- Credit card systems for card account closures
- Loan systems for mortgage and loan payoff handling
- Investment systems for securities and brokerage accounts

Each of these systems may have been built at different times, by different vendors, using different technologies. They may store data in different formats, use different customer identifiers, and require different authentication mechanisms. Connecting them all into a coherent estate processing workflow requires navigating the entire spaghetti landscape.

This is why estate processing so often relies on manual workarounds. It's not that institutions don't want to automate. It's that automation would require building integrations across a dozen or more legacy systems, integrations that are expensive to build, fragile to maintain, and likely to break whenever any underlying system changes.

The Vendor Dependency

Compounding the technology debt is the reality of vendor relationships in banking.

Most institutions don't build their own core banking systems. They buy them from vendors, large players like FIS, Fiserv, Jack Henry, Temenos, and others who specialize in banking technology. These vendor relationships provide stability and shared development costs, but they also create dependencies.

When your core banking system is a vendor product, your ability to change that system depends on the vendor's roadmap, the vendor's priorities, and the vendor's willingness to accommodate your specific needs. Estate processing may be important to you, but if it's not important to enough of the vendor's customer base, improvements won't be prioritized.

Vendor contracts can lock institutions into multi-year agreements with limited flexibility. Switching vendors is an enormous undertaking, the Commonwealth Bank of Australia's core system replacement took five years and cost approximately $750 million. Most institutions simply can't contemplate such a transition. They're locked into their current platforms for the foreseeable future.

This means that even when institutions want to improve estate processing, they may lack the technical latitude to do so. The core system doesn't support the workflow they need. The vendor doesn't offer the integration they require. The customization would void their support agreement. They're trapped by dependencies they created years or decades ago.

What Technology Debt Costs Estate Processing

Let me make this concrete. Here's how technology debt affects your estate processing operations:

No unified customer view. When a death notification arrives, the estate services team should be able to see everything: all accounts, all products, all beneficiary designations, all relevant documents. But if customer data is scattered across fifteen systems with no integration layer, building that unified view is impossible. The team must log into system after system, manually assembling the picture. Information gets missed. Errors occur.

Manual document handling. Modern document management should allow digital documents to flow automatically into case files, be tagged with metadata, and be accessible from any relevant system. But if your document management system doesn't integrate with your case management system, someone must manually download documents, rename them, and upload them elsewhere. If your scanning system uses a different identifier than your case management system, someone must manually match documents to cases.

No workflow automation. A modern case management system should automatically route work, send notifications, track deadlines, and escalate delays. But if your case management system can't talk to your core banking system, how does it know when accounts have been reviewed? If it can't talk to your correspondence system, how does it trigger letters? Without integration, workflow automation is impossible. Humans must manually track status, manually send notifications, manually chase deadlines.

Duplicate data entry. When systems don't integrate, humans become the integration layer. The same information, the date of death, the executor's name, the account numbers, gets entered repeatedly into different systems. Every re-entry is an opportunity for error. Every re-entry is wasted time.

Limited reporting. If your systems don't share data, how do you report on estate processing performance? You can't measure what you can't see. The metrics that would help you improve, average processing time, error rates, customer satisfaction, require data from multiple systems. Without integration, that data doesn't exist in any combined form.

Inability to innovate. Even if you wanted to offer beneficiaries an online portal to track their case status, how would you build it? The portal would need to pull data from case management, document management, and core banking, systems that may have no modern API layer, no way to expose data to external applications. Innovation requires integration, and integration requires architecture that supports it.

This is the estate processing tax imposed by technology debt. It's not visible on any financial statement, but it's real and substantial. It shows up in staff hours wasted on manual workarounds, in errors that require correction, in customer complaints that require response, and in beneficiaries who leave because the experience was unacceptable.

The Modernization Trap

Given the costs of technology debt, why don't institutions simply modernize?

The short answer: risk.

Core banking systems are precisely that, core. They process every transaction, hold every balance, maintain every customer record. They can't fail. Any disruption, even briefly, has immediate and severe consequences: customers unable to access funds, payments failing, regulatory violations, reputational damage.

The risk of modernization isn't theoretical. TSB Bank's 2018 IT migration in the UK left 1.9 million customers unable to access their accounts for weeks. The bank's CEO resigned. Regulators imposed massive fines. The reputational damage was substantial and lasting.

A large US bank experienced significant system failures in February 2019 due to issues with its legacy infrastructure, causing widespread disruptions and preventing customers from accessing online banking, ATMs, and mobile banking services. The incident demonstrated how tightly interconnected banking systems have become, and how devastating failures can be.

These examples make bank executives understandably cautious. The systems they have may be expensive to maintain, difficult to change, and limiting to innovation, but they work. They process transactions reliably, day after day. The devil you know is preferable to the devil of a failed migration.

This creates the modernization trap. The longer you wait to modernize, the more technical debt accumulates, the more expensive and risky modernization becomes, and the less likely you're to attempt it. Institutions can become paralyzed, spending ever-increasing sums to maintain systems they know are inadequate but are afraid to replace.

The Estate Processing Implications

Estate processing sits at the intersection of all these technology challenges.

It's not a revenue-generating function that might justify its own modernization investment. It touches too many systems to be easily isolated and improved in pieces. It serves a population, bereaved families, who have no market power to demand better technology. And it happens infrequently enough that its problems don't create the kind of visible, urgent crises that force institutional attention.

The result is that estate processing often runs on the oldest, least integrated, most manual layers of the technology stack. When newer systems are built, estate processing is an afterthought. When integration projects are prioritized, estate processing is at the bottom of the list. When automation initiatives are funded, estate processing is overlooked.

This isn't because institutions don't care about bereaved families. It's because technology investment follows business priorities, and estate processing, invisible, unquantified, organizationally homeless, doesn't compete effectively for resources.

Breaking the Impasse

The technology challenges facing estate processing are real but not insurmountable. Institutions can make progress without requiring massive core system replacements. The key is targeting investments strategically.

Strategy 1: The API Layer

Instead of replacing legacy systems, wrap them in modern APIs. An application programming interface, commonly called an API, creates a standardized way for different software systems to talk to each other. In practice, it provides access to data and functionality in a legacy system without modifying the system itself.

For estate processing, this might mean creating APIs that expose customer account data, document storage, and case status information. These APIs can then feed a modern case management application that sits on top of the legacy infrastructure. The core systems continue running unchanged; the API layer translates between old and new.

This approach is sometimes called "progressive modernization" modernizing the interface while preserving the underlying systems. It's lower risk than replacement and can deliver benefits incrementally.

Strategy 2: The Workflow Platform

Modern workflow and case management platforms can orchestrate processes across multiple legacy systems. Instead of requiring tight integration between systems, these platforms can manage handoffs through a combination of APIs, file transfers, and even manual tasks assigned to users.

Wells Fargo's Estate Care Centre implemented this approach using Pegasystems workflow software. The platform creates case files automatically, tracks status across departments, and ensures that families don't have to repeat their stories, even though the underlying banking systems remain separate.

The workflow platform doesn't eliminate the need for eventual integration, but it provides immediate benefits: better visibility, consistent process, reduced errors, and improved customer experience.

Strategy 3: The Data Hub

If your estate services team needs data from twelve different systems, building twelve separate integrations is expensive and fragile. An alternative is a data hub, a centralized layer that collects and consolidates data from multiple sources, making it accessible through a single interface.

For estate processing, a data hub could aggregate customer data, account information, and case status into a unified view. When a death notification arrives, the estate specialist sees everything in one place, even though the underlying data lives in disparate systems.

Data hubs don't require modifying source systems; they read data through whatever interfaces are available (APIs, database queries, file exports). They can be built incrementally, adding sources as integration work proceeds.

Strategy 4: The RPA Stopgap

Robotic Process Automation, often called RPA, uses software "bots" to perform tasks that humans currently do manually, logging into systems, copying data between applications, filling out forms, sending notifications.

RPA isn't a long-term solution; it automates manual workarounds rather than eliminating them. But it can provide immediate relief while more fundamental modernization proceeds. If your estate services team currently spends hours per case navigating between systems, RPA can reduce that time significantly, freeing staff for higher-value work.

The danger of RPA is that it can become a crutch, reducing the urgency of real modernization. Used strategically, it buys time. Used indiscriminately, it embeds inefficiency. AI can also be explored here since it's more efficient and faster than RPA.

Strategy 5: The Targeted Replacement

Not all systems are equally critical or equally difficult to replace. Some components of the estate processing workflow may be candidates for targeted replacement, removing a specific legacy system and substituting a modern alternative.

Document management is often a good candidate. Modern document management systems offer cloud storage, automatic optical character recognition (which converts scanned documents into searchable text), intelligent categorization, and integration-friendly APIs. Replacing a legacy document management system can deliver immediate benefits to estate processing without touching the core banking platform.

Case management is another candidate. Modern case management platforms are designed for complex, multi-step processes that span departments and systems. They're built for exactly the kind of workflow that estate processing requires.

The key is selecting targets carefully, systems where replacement is feasible, risk is manageable, and benefits to estate processing are clear.

The Business Case for Technology Investment

How do you justify technology investment in estate processing when the ROI isn't immediately obvious?

Start by quantifying the current costs:

Labor costs. How many staff hours are consumed by estate processing? What's the fully-loaded cost of that labor? How much of that time is spent on manual workarounds that automation could eliminate?

Error costs. How many estate-related errors occur annually? What does it cost to correct them, in staff time, customer compensation, regulatory response?

Customer experience costs. What's your estate-related complaint rate? How much staff time goes to handling complaints? What's the reputational damage of poor reviews and negative word-of-mouth?

Retention costs. This is the biggest number, though the hardest to quantify precisely. Based on the data from Chapter 3, what percentage of inherited assets leave your institution? What's that worth in lost deposits, lost fee income, lost lending relationships?

Now estimate the benefits of improvement:

Labor savings. If automation reduced estate processing time by 50%, how many staff hours would that free? What could those hours be redeployed to?

Error reduction. If a modern workflow system reduced errors by 75%, what would that save in correction costs?

Experience improvement. If processing time dropped from 90 days to 30 days, and beneficiaries received proactive updates throughout, how would complaint rates change?

Retention improvement. If improved processing increased beneficiary retention by 10 percentage points, what would that mean in retained deposits?

The numbers will vary by institution, but the general pattern holds: the hidden costs of current estate processing are substantial, and the potential benefits of improvement are significant. Technology investment isn't charity; it's arithmetic.

The Leadership Imperative

Technology debt is a leadership issue, not just an IT issue.

Deloitte makes this point directly: "Modernization is a strategic business issue, not a technology issue. If you throw the task over the wall to IT, you will probably just end up with updated apps (after waiting two or three years)."

The institutions that successfully address technology debt do so because senior leadership makes it a priority. They set clear direction, allocate resources, manage risk, and hold teams accountable. They understand that the gap between their institution and more agile competitors grows wider every day they delay.

Estate processing modernization won't happen because the IT department decides it's important. It will happen because the CEO, the COO, and the board recognize that estate processing is a strategic vulnerability, a failure of customer experience, a driver of attrition, and an operational burden that grows heavier each year.

The question leadership must answer is direct: Can you afford to keep spending 70% of your technology budget maintaining yesterday's systems while your ability to serve customers erodes? Can you afford to watch beneficiaries leave because your processes are too slow, too manual, too frustrating? Can you afford to fall further behind institutions that have invested in modern capabilities?

The costs of technology debt are hidden, but they're real. The question is whether you'll address them before they become impossible to ignore.

CHAPTER SEVEN

The Estate Readiness Opportunity

For six chapters, we've examined what's broken: the demographic wave, the estate processing ordeal, the retention crisis, the regulatory complexity, the operational tangle, the technology debt. The diagnosis is complete. The patient isn't healthy.

This is where the conversation shifts from diagnosis to action.

This chapter begins Part Three: The Opportunity. We're moving from what's wrong to what's possible, from the cost of failure to the value of transformation. We're moving from estate processing (a reactive function) to Estate Readiness (a proactive strategy).

That distinction matters more than most executives realize.

The Reactive Default

Consider how most financial institutions currently approach customer death:

A customer dies. A family member shows up at a branch or calls a phone number. The institution learns of the death. Systems are frozen. Processes begin. Documents are requested. Weeks pass. More documents are requested. More weeks pass. Eventually, the estate is settled. The beneficiaries, who have had a frustrating, time-consuming experience, make decisions about where to bank going forward.

This is reactive estate processing. The institution waits for death to happen and then responds. Every action occurs after the fact. Every interaction is remedial. The institution is perpetually catching up, perpetually responding to a situation that has already occurred.

In a reactive model, the institution has no relationship with beneficiaries before they inherit. It has no insight into the customer's wishes, the family structure, or the complexity of the estate. It has collected no documents in advance, established no expectations, built no trust with the next generation.

The reactive model treats death as an exception, an unwelcome interruption to normal business that must be managed and resolved. It's defensive rather than strategic, administrative rather than relational.

And it's the model that produces the outcomes we've documented: 80% of heirs changing advisors, 70% of widows leaving within a year, average processing times of 6 - 9 months, endemic family frustration, and billions of dollars in departed deposits.

The Estate Readiness Alternative

Now consider a different approach.

A customer opens accounts at your institution. Over the years, as part of your relationship with that customer, you help them prepare for the eventual transfer of their assets. You ensure beneficiary designations are current and complete. You collect information about family members. You store important documents securely. You introduce the customer's children to your institution. You discuss their wishes and document their preferences.

When the customer eventually passes, your institution is prepared. You already know who the beneficiaries are. You already have their contact information. You may already have a relationship with them. You have the documents you need, or you know exactly what's missing. You can reach out proactively, with compassion and competence, rather than waiting for a confused family member to figure out whom to call.

The estate settles quickly, not because death has become simpler, but because the preparation was done in advance. The beneficiaries, who have been treated with care throughout, see your institution as a partner in a difficult time rather than an obstacle to overcome. They're more likely to keep their inherited assets with you. They're more likely to consolidate their existing accounts. They're more likely to recommend you to others.

This is Estate Readiness: a proactive strategy that treats wealth transfer not as an exception to be managed but as a lifecycle stage to be served.

The Business Case for Proactivity

Why should institutions invest in Estate Readiness? Because the economics are compelling.

Processing Cost Reduction

When beneficiary designations are complete and current, accounts transfer directly, no probate, no court documents, no Letters Testamentary required for those accounts. When family information is already on file, intake happens faster. When documents are pre-collected, verification happens immediately.

Every hour saved in estate processing is an hour of staff time freed for other work. If your institution currently spends 8 hours per estate case, and proactive preparation could reduce that to 4 hours, you've cut processing costs in half. At 500 estates per year, that's 2,000 hours, approximately one full-time employee, recovered annually.

Error Reduction

Estate processing errors are expensive. They require correction, generate complaints, and occasionally create legal exposure. Errors often result from incomplete information, rushed processing, or unfamiliarity with the customer's situation.

When estate preparation happens during the customer's lifetime, there's time to get things right. Beneficiary designations can be reviewed and verified. Questions can be asked and answered. Ambiguities can be resolved. The result is fewer errors, fewer corrections, and fewer complaints.

Customer Experience Improvement

Estate experience is the experience that determines whether relationships continue. A family that has a good experience during estate settlement becomes a loyal customer. A family that has a bad experience leaves, and tells others.

Proactive preparation transforms estate experience. Instead of confusion about what's needed, families receive clear guidance. Instead of weeks of waiting, processing moves quickly. Instead of bureaucratic indifference, families feel cared for. The experience differential is enormous.

Retention Improvement

This is the core business case. As we established in Chapter 3, the current estate processing model hemorrhages beneficiaries. Proactive Estate Readiness reverses the dynamic.

When you have a relationship with beneficiaries before they inherit, they're more likely to stay. When the estate process is smooth and supportive, they're more likely to stay. When they see your institution as a partner in their family's financial life, they're more likely to stay.

If Estate Readiness can improve beneficiary retention by even 10-15 percentage points, bringing it from, say, 40% to 50-55%, the revenue impact is substantial. For a mid-sized institution with $3 billion in deposits and 2,500 annual deaths in the customer base, a 15% improvement in retention could mean $20-30 million in additional retained deposits per year. That's not a one-time benefit; it compounds as the wealth transfer wave continues.

The Three Pillars of Estate Readiness

In Chapters 4, 5, and 6, we examined the constraints that make estate processing difficult: regulatory complexity, operational fragmentation, and technology debt. Estate Readiness must address all three, not by eliminating constraints, but by building capabilities that work within them.

This requires attention to three interconnected pillars: Planning, Documentation, and Execution.

Planning: Helping Customers Prepare

The first pillar is enabling customers to plan effectively for wealth transfer during their lifetimes. This means:

- Ensuring beneficiary designations are complete and current across all eligible accounts
- Mapping family relationships so the institution understands who will inherit and what relationships already exist
- Facilitating conversations about estate intentions, even when those conversations are uncomfortable

- Connecting customers with estate planning professionals when specialized guidance is needed

Planning addresses the root cause of estate processing difficulty. When customers have planned well, their estates are simpler to settle. When beneficiary designations are in place, accounts transfer directly. When family relationships are documented, outreach is immediate and informed.

Documentation: Capturing and Storing Critical Information

The second pillar is documentation, gathering the information and documents that will be needed when the customer passes and storing them securely until that time.

Recall from Chapter 5 the documentation challenges in estate processing: death certificates arrive separately from case files, Letters Testamentary must be matched to existing cases, beneficiary identification must be collected and verified. Much of this work could be done in advance, but institutions lack the infrastructure to collect and store documents during the customer's lifetime.

Effective documentation infrastructure includes:

- Secure digital storage for estate-related documents (wills, trusts, powers of attorney)
- Beneficiary contact information and identification captured in advance
- Customer wishes and instructions recorded and accessible
- Integration with estate processing workflows so pre-collected information flows automatically to processing teams

Documentation infrastructure transforms estate processing from a scavenger hunt into an organized retrieval. Instead of chasing documents across departments and systems, processing teams access what they need from a central, secure repository.

Execution: Orchestrating the Estate Settlement Process

The third pillar is execution, the actual process of settling estates when customers pass. This is where the operational and technology challenges we examined in Chapters 5 and 6 must be addressed.

Effective execution requires:

- Workflow orchestration that coordinates across departments and systems
- Automated notifications and status updates that keep families informed
- Single points of contact who guide families through the process
- Integration with core banking, document management, and case management systems

The execution pillar is where planning and documentation pay off. When preparation has been done well, execution becomes dramatically simpler. When documentation is pre-collected, verification is immediate. When family relationships are mapped, outreach is informed and personal.

These three pillars are interconnected. Planning without documentation leaves good intentions unrecorded. Documentation without execution leaves collected information unused. Execution without planning and documentation is the reactive model we're trying to escape.

The Infrastructure Approach

Estate Readiness isn't a program you can implement through policy changes and staff training alone. It requires infrastructure, technology capabilities that enable planning, documentation, and execution at scale.

This is where many institutions struggle. As we discussed in Chapter 6, legacy core banking systems weren't designed for estate processing. Document management systems don't integrate with case management. Customer data is siloed across departments. Building the infrastructure for Estate Readiness seems to require solving all of these problems at once.

But there's an alternative approach: purpose-built infrastructure that sits alongside existing systems rather than requiring their replacement.

Prismm was built on this exact premise. Rather than asking institutions to modernize their entire technology stack before addressing estate readiness, the Prismm platform provides inheritance infrastructure that integrates with existing systems, connecting the dots between planning, documentation, and execution without requiring massive core system transformation.

An effective estate orchestration platform functions as a digital vault and coordination layer, approaching the problem from an infrastructure perspective. At its best, this kind of platform enables:

- **Document pre-collection and secure storage**. Customers can store estate-related documents in a secure digital vault, accessible to the institution when needed for estate processing. This addresses the documentation pillar directly.
- **Beneficiary designation management.** The platform tracks beneficiary designations across accounts, identifies gaps, and prompts reviews, ensuring that accounts are ready for direct transfer when the time comes.
- **Family relationship mapping.** Rather than treating customers as isolated individuals, the platform maps family relationships, identifying beneficiaries, their contact information, and their existing relationships with the institution.
- **Life event verification.** When a customer passes, the platform provides verification infrastructure that streamlines the death notification and documentation process, addressing the regulatory requirements we outlined in Chapter 4 while reducing the manual effort documented in Chapter 5.
- **Workflow orchestration**. The platform coordinates estate processing workflows across departments, reducing the handoff problems we identified in Chapter 5. Instead of 21 separate handoffs, processing flows through an integrated system that maintains context and accountability.

The infrastructure approach is significant because it addresses the technology debt challenge without requiring institutions to first solve that challenge. Recall from Chapter 6 that banks spend 60-80% of their IT budgets maintaining existing systems, leaving little capacity for innovation. Purpose-built inheritance infrastructure provides Estate Readiness capabilities without competing for those constrained modernization resources.

You don't need to replace your core banking system to implement Estate Readiness. You need infrastructure that works with your existing systems while providing the capabilities those systems lack.

This is where the economics start working in your favor. By deploying purpose-built inheritance infrastructure, institutions can achieve Estate Readiness outcomes without the multi-year, multi-million-dollar technology transformations that would otherwise be required.

The Trust Dimension

Estate Readiness has a trust dimension that extends beyond technology and process.

When customers entrust your institution with their estate planning documents, their family information, their wishes and intentions, they're placing extraordinary trust in you. They're saying: "I trust you to care for my family when I'm no longer here to care for them myself."

This trust creates both obligation and opportunity.

The obligation is to handle that trust with the utmost care. Security must be impeccable. Privacy must be protected. Access controls must be robust. When families retrieve information after a customer's death, they must find exactly what they expect, exactly where they expect it.

The opportunity is that trust, once established, is difficult for competitors to dislodge. A customer who has invested in estate preparation with your institution, who has stored documents, designated beneficiaries, introduced family members, and documented wishes, is deeply engaged. That engagement creates loyalty that transcends rate competition and product features.

Trust also extends across generations. When beneficiaries inherit into an institution that handled their parent's or grandparent's estate with competence and care, they inherit trust along with assets. They've seen your institution at its best, serving their family during a difficult time. That experience becomes the foundation of their own relationship with you.

The institutions that excel at Estate Readiness will be those that recognize this trust dimension and treat it with the seriousness it deserves. They'll invest in security, in privacy, in the careful handling of sensitive information. They'll train their staff to approach estate conversations with appropriate gravity. They'll earn trust through competence, and they'll retain it through care.

Purpose-built inheritance infrastructure is built on this trust foundation. Designed specifically for financial institutions, it incorporates the security, compliance, and access controls that banking requires, while providing the functionality that estate readiness demands. The platform becomes an extension of the institution's existing trust relationship with customers, not a separate service that customers must learn to trust independently.

The Customer Conversation

Estate Readiness requires talking about death, a topic that many people avoid and many institutions are reluctant to raise.

This is understandable. Death is uncomfortable. Customers don't want to think about it. Bankers don't want to seem morbid or intrusive. It's easier to focus on everyday transactions, investments, loans, and the business of living.

But avoidance comes at a cost. When customers don't prepare, their families suffer. When institutions don't help, they lose the opportunity to serve and retain. The discomfort of conversation is far smaller than the cost of its absence.

Research from wealth management firms consistently shows that many clients put off thinking about wealth transfer plans until an emergency forces the conversation. But by then, it may be too late. Planning early allows time for building relationships with family members, developing financial literacy in the next generation, and ensuring clear understanding of objectives and values.

The key is framing. Estate preparation isn't about death; it's about care. It's about ensuring that customers' wishes are honored, that their families are provided for, that the wealth they've built serves the purposes they intend. It's about control, maintaining control even when the customer is no longer present to exercise it directly.

Customers, when approached thoughtfully, are often grateful for the conversation. They know they should prepare. They know their documents are outdated or incomplete. They just need permission and support to address something they've been avoiding.

The most effective conversations happen in the context of life events:

- A new grandchild is born: "Have you thought about updating your beneficiary designations to include your grandchildren?"

- A customer retires: "As you enter this new phase, it's a good time to review your estate plan. Is everything up to date?"
- A spouse passes: "I know this is a difficult time. When you're ready, we should review your own plans and make sure everything reflects your current wishes."

These moments provide natural openings for estate conversations without requiring the institution to raise the topic out of the blue. They connect preparation to life, not death.

Next-Generation Engagement

The heirs who will inherit your customers' wealth are, in many cases, completely unknown to your institution. They bank elsewhere. They've never set foot in your branches. They have no relationship with you and no particular reason to maintain one after they inherit.

This is a strategic vulnerability. Research from Cerulli Associates shows that 89% of high-net-worth firms now cite family-focused services as a top growth strategy, recognizing that multi-generational relationships are essential to surviving the wealth transfer wave.

Next-generation engagement changes the equation. By building relationships with beneficiaries before inheritance, you create continuity that survives the wealth transfer.

Next-generation engagement takes many forms:

- **Family meetings.** Invite customers to bring their adult children to meetings with relationship managers. Discuss the family's financial situation, the estate plan, and how the institution can serve multiple generations.
- **Financial education.** Offer educational programs for younger customers: financial literacy workshops, homebuying seminars, investment basics. These programs build relationships while providing genuine value.
- **Youth accounts.** Encourage customers to open accounts for children and grandchildren. A child who grows up with your

institution is more likely to stay, and more likely to consolidate inherited assets with existing accounts.

- **Beneficiary awareness.** When a customer designates a beneficiary, ensure that beneficiary knows they've been named and understands what will happen when they eventually inherit.

The wealth management industry has learned this lesson through painful experience. When advisors fail to engage heirs during the client's lifetime, assets flee at inheritance. When advisors take the time to build meaningful relationships with heirs, retention rates double or more.

Banks and credit unions face the same dynamic. The institutions that engage multiple generations will retain assets. The institutions that don't will watch wealth walk out the door.

The Institutional Commitment

Estate Readiness isn't a program you can launch and forget. It's not a set of checklists to complete or metrics to report. It's a cultural commitment, a decision to treat wealth transfer as a core business function deserving sustained attention.

This commitment has several dimensions:

Executive sponsorship. Estate Readiness requires senior leadership to champion it. Without executive support, the initiative will be deprioritized when resources are tight, metrics will go unreported, and momentum will fade.

Cross-functional ownership. Estate Readiness touches multiple departments: retail banking, wealth management, operations, compliance, IT. It can't live in any single department; it requires coordination across organizational boundaries. As we discussed in Chapter 5, siloed organizations struggle to deliver coherent customer experiences. Estate Readiness requires breaking down those silos.

Incentive alignment. Front-line employees will focus on what they're measured on. If relationship managers are measured only on new account acquisition, they won't invest time in beneficiary reviews. Estate Readiness requires incorporating estate-related activities into performance expectations.

Sustained investment. Building Estate Readiness capabilities takes time and resources. Technology must be deployed, processes must be redesigned, training must be delivered. This investment must be sustained over years, not abandoned after an initial burst of enthusiasm.

Customer education. Estate Readiness only works if customers participate. They need to understand why preparation matters, what your institution offers, and how to take action. This requires ongoing communication through multiple channels.

The institutions that succeed at Estate Readiness will be those that treat it not as a project but as a permanent strategic priority, a way of doing business that becomes embedded in culture, process, and technology.

The Competitive Advantage

Estate Readiness isn't yet standard practice in the financial services industry. Most institutions still operate in reactive mode, processing estates after the fact rather than preparing for them in advance. This creates an opportunity for differentiation.

The institution that becomes known for helping customers prepare, and for serving families with exceptional care when death occurs, gains a competitive advantage that's difficult to replicate. It's an advantage built on trust, on relationships, on demonstrated competence in moments that matter most.

This advantage manifests in multiple ways:

Customer acquisition. Customers seeking comprehensive financial partners will be attracted to an institution that offers estate readiness support. It signals sophistication, care, and long-term thinking.

Customer retention. Customers who have invested in estate preparation with your institution are deeply engaged. They've entrusted you with sensitive information and important decisions. That engagement creates loyalty that transcends product features and rate competition.

Beneficiary retention. This is the core prize. When beneficiaries inherit, they inherit into a relationship. They inherit into processes that work smoothly. They inherit into an institution that has already demonstrated care for their family. They're far more likely to stay.

Referral generation. Families served well during estate settlement become advocates. They tell friends, colleagues, and extended family about their experience. They recommend your institution to others facing similar situations.

The competitive advantage of Estate Readiness is nearly impossible to replicate quickly. It requires years of investment, genuine cultural commitment, and accumulated expertise. An institution that starts now builds a lead that competitors will struggle to close.

Getting Started

Estate Readiness may sound daunting. Start small anyway. You don't need to build every capability at once. You don't need to transform your institution overnight. You need to begin.

Start with beneficiary designations. This is the highest-leverage intervention. Audit your current designation rates. Identify gaps. Build outreach programs. Track improvement. This single initiative, executed well, can dramatically improve estate outcomes.

Payable-on-death (POD) and transfer-on-death (TOD) designations allow accounts to bypass the probate process entirely. When these designations are in place and current, estate settlement becomes dramatically simpler, the beneficiary presents a death certificate and identification, and the funds transfer. No court documents required. No waiting for probate.

Start with customer conversations. Train relationship managers to discuss estate preparation naturally. Provide them with conversation guides and educational materials. Celebrate examples of effective customer engagement.

Start with one segment. Perhaps you focus on customers over 65 with significant balances. Perhaps you focus on customers who have recently experienced a spouse's death. Concentrating resources on a defined population allows you to learn before scaling.

Start with infrastructure. Purpose-built inheritance infrastructure can accelerate your Estate Readiness journey by providing the planning, documentation, and execution capabilities your legacy systems lack. Rather than waiting years to modernize core systems, you can deploy infrastructure that integrates with what you have today, addressing the technology constraints outlined in Chapter 6 without requiring their full resolution.

The goal is progress, not perfection. Every beneficiary designation completed, every family relationship documented, every next-generation conversation held, these are building blocks. They accumulate. Over time, they transform your institution's readiness for the wealth transfer wave.

The Stakes

The great wealth transfer isn't a distant future. It's happening now. Every day, 10,000 Baby Boomers cross the threshold of age 65. Every year, 2.8 million Americans die, a number that will grow to 3.6 million annually by 2037. Cerulli Associates projects that $84 trillion will transfer to heirs through 2045, with an additional $21 trillion directed to charity.

Institutions that are ready, truly ready, will capture disproportionate value from this transition. They'll retain assets that competitors lose. They'll build relationships that span generations. They'll establish reputations that attract customers seeking competent, caring financial partners.

Institutions that aren't ready will watch wealth walk out the door. They'll process estates slowly and painfully. They'll frustrate families at moments of maximum vulnerability. They'll wonder, years from now, why their deposit base is shrinking and their customer base is aging.

Studies consistently show that only about one-third of Americans have any estate plan at all. Without proper planning, wealth may be lost to taxes, legal fees, or family disputes. The institution that helps customers prepare, that makes preparation easy, accessible, and integrated with their banking relationship, provides genuine value while building strategic advantage.

Estate Readiness is a choice. It's a choice about whether to treat wealth transfer as a problem to be managed or an opportunity to be seized. It's a choice about whether to remain reactive or to become proactive. It's a choice about what kind of institution you want to be.

The direction you choose will define your institution for the next two decades.

Estate Readiness Self-Assessment

Use these questions to evaluate your institution's current state and identify priorities:

Planning Pillar

- What percentage of eligible accounts have complete beneficiary designations?
- When were those designations last reviewed or updated?
- How easy is it for customers to add or update beneficiaries?
- Do you prompt beneficiary reviews after life events?
- Do you facilitate family conversations about estate intentions?

Documentation Pillar

- Do you offer customers secure document storage?
- What documents do you collect during the customer's lifetime?
- Is pre-collected information accessible to estate processing teams?
- Do customers understand the value of document pre-collection?
- Is document storage integrated with your estate processing workflows?

Execution Pillar

- Can you identify family relationships in your customer data?
- When a customer dies, can you immediately identify beneficiaries and their contact information?
- Do you have workflow orchestration across estate processing functions?
- Do families receive proactive status updates?
- Do you track estate processing metrics (cycle time, errors, satisfaction)?

Next-Generation Engagement

- Do you actively build relationships with customers' adult children?
- Do you offer financial education programs for younger generations?
- Do you encourage youth accounts and family account linkages?
- What percentage of beneficiaries are already customers when they inherit?

Infrastructure Readiness

- Have you deployed purpose-built inheritance infrastructure?
- Does your infrastructure integrate with your existing core systems?
- Can you address planning, documentation, and execution through a unified platform?
- Does your infrastructure support the regulatory requirements outlined in Chapter 4?
- Does your infrastructure reduce the operational handoffs identified in Chapter 5?

Organizational Commitment

- Who owns Estate Readiness at the executive level?
- How is performance measured and reported?
- Are front-line employees incentivized for estate-related activities?
- What investment has been made in capabilities and training?

CHAPTER EIGHT

The Transformation Playbook

Understanding the Estate Readiness opportunity is one thing. Capturing it is another.

The previous chapter laid out what Estate Readiness looks like: the three pillars of Planning, Documentation, and Execution; the infrastructure approach; the trust dimension; the customer conversation. But understanding the destination doesn't mean you know how to get there.

This chapter is the playbook, the practical guide for transforming your institution from reactive estate processing to proactive Estate Readiness. It addresses the questions that keep executives awake at night: Where do we start? How do we build momentum? What does the implementation timeline look like? How do we measure success? How do we sustain commitment when competing priorities emerge?

Transformation is hard. Research consistently shows that 70% of transformation initiatives fail to achieve their intended objectives. The failures aren't usually technical, they're organizational. They're failures of commitment, of change management, of sustained attention. This chapter will help you avoid those failures.

The Transformation Mindset

Before diving into tactics, let's establish the right mindset.

Estate Readiness transformation isn't a technology project with a beginning, middle, and end. It's not something you "complete." It's a permanent shift in how your institution thinks about customer relationships and lifecycle management.

This distinction matters because it shapes how you approach the work.

A project mindset leads to temporary attention, a burst of investment, and then a return to "normal operations." The project team disbands. Metrics stop being tracked. Enthusiasm fades. Within 18 months, you're back where you started, processing estates reactively, losing beneficiaries, wondering why the initiative didn't stick.

A transformation mindset recognizes that you're changing the way your institution operates. You're building new capabilities, establishing new processes, shifting cultural expectations. This takes years, not months. It requires sustained leadership attention, not a one-time executive announcement. It demands continuous improvement, not a single implementation milestone.

The institutions that succeed at Estate Readiness will be those that approach it as ongoing strategic priority, embedded in how they serve customers, measure performance, and allocate resources, not as a discrete project to be checked off a list.

Phase One: Assessment and Foundation (Months 1-3)

Every transformation begins with understanding where you are. You can't plot a course without knowing your starting point.

Assess Your Current State

Start by mapping your existing estate processing operations. This means documenting:

- How are deaths currently reported to your institution?
- What happens when a death notification arrives, who isn't notified, what systems are updated, what processes are triggered?
- How many handoffs occur between notification and estate settlement?
- What documents are required and when they're requested?
- How long estates take to settle? (not what you think, what your data actually shows)
- What errors occur most frequently?
- What complaints families register most often?

This mapping exercise often reveals surprises. Institutions discover processes they didn't know existed, handoffs that add weeks without adding value, and system gaps that force manual workarounds. One institution found that death certificates were being faxed between departments because the document management system couldn't handle the workflow, a workaround that had persisted for eight years without anyone questioning it.

Quantify the Opportunity

Next, build the business case with real numbers from your institution:

- How many customer deaths do you process annually?
- What is your current beneficiary retention rate? (If you don't know, that's your first finding.)
- What is the average deposit balance of customers who die?
- What percentage of that balance departs within 12 months?
- What are the fully loaded costs of estate processing, staff time, error correction, customer complaints, regulatory responses?

These numbers create urgency. When executives see that $50 million in deposits walks out the door annually because of poor estate experience, Estate Readiness stops being a "nice to have" and becomes a strategic imperative.

Audit Your Beneficiary Designations

Beneficiary designation completeness is the single most actionable metric for Estate Readiness. Payable-on-death (POD) and transfer-on-death (TOD) designations allow accounts to bypass the probate process entirely, the beneficiary presents a death certificate and identification, and funds transfer directly.

Audit your current state:

- What percentage of eligible accounts have beneficiary designations?
- When were those designations last reviewed or updated?
- What percentage of designations are clearly outdated (deceased beneficiaries, ex-spouses, etc.)?

Most institutions find that 30-40% of eligible accounts lack any beneficiary designation, and another 20-30% have designations that haven't been reviewed in over five years. This represents both a problem and an opportunity, every designation gap closed is an estate settlement simplified.

Secure Executive Sponsorship

Research on organizational change consistently identifies executive sponsorship as the single greatest contributor to transformation success. Conversely, lack of executive support is the primary obstacle to success.

Estate Readiness requires a senior executive sponsor, ideally someone at the C-suite level, who will:

- Champion the initiative publicly and repeatedly
- Allocate resources (budget, people, technology)
- Remove organizational obstacles
- Hold leaders accountable for results
- Model the behaviors the transformation requires

The sponsor doesn't need to manage the day-to-day work, but they need to be visibly engaged. They need to attend key meetings, ask about progress in leadership forums, celebrate early wins, and address resistance directly. Without this visible commitment, the organization will conclude that Estate Readiness isn't really a priority, and they'll act accordingly.

Establish Cross-Functional Ownership

Estate processing touches multiple departments: retail banking, operations, compliance, wealth management, IT, customer service. No single department can transform the end-to-end experience alone.

Establish a cross-functional steering committee with representatives from each affected area. Give them clear authority to make decisions, resolve conflicts, and drive progress. Meet regularly, weekly during intensive implementation phases, monthly during steady-state operations.

Avoid the temptation to house the initiative entirely within one department. If Estate Readiness lives in operations, the customer experience elements will be neglected. If it lives in retail banking, the compliance requirements will be underweighted. If it lives in IT, the human dimensions will be overlooked. Cross-functional governance ensures balanced attention.

Phase Two: Quick Wins and Proof Points (Months 3-6)

Transformation requires momentum, and momentum requires early victories. Before launching comprehensive change, identify quick wins that demonstrate value and build organizational confidence.

Launch a Beneficiary Designation Campaign

The fastest path to Estate Readiness improvement is increasing beneficiary designation rates. This requires no technology investment, no process redesign, no regulatory approval, just focused attention.

Design an outreach campaign targeting customers with eligible accounts lacking beneficiary designations. Start with your highest-value customers: those over 65 with significant balances. These are the customers most likely to have estate events soon and whose accounts will benefit most from simplified transfer.

Train relationship managers to have beneficiary conversations. Provide scripts, talking points, and educational materials. Track designation completion rates by branch, by relationship manager, by customer segment. Celebrate progress publicly.

A well-executed beneficiary campaign can increase designation rates by 15-20 percentage points within six months, a meaningful improvement in estate readiness that delivers value immediately and builds momentum for broader transformation.

Pilot Customer Conversations

Estate planning conversations are unfamiliar territory for most bankers. Before rolling out institution-wide, pilot the approach with a small group of relationship managers who are comfortable with the topic and eager to try something new.

Select 5-10 relationship managers across different branches. Train them in estate conversation techniques. Provide conversation guides and educational materials they can share with customers. Set expectations: you're not asking them to become estate planning experts, just to open conversations about preparation and connect customers with relevant resources.

Track what works. Which conversation openers resonate? What objections arise? Which customers are most receptive? What follow-up materials do relationship managers wish they had?

After three months, debrief thoroughly. Refine the approach based on real experience. Then you're ready to scale.

Measure and Report

What gets measured gets managed. From the beginning of your transformation, establish metrics and reporting cadence:

- Beneficiary designation completion rate (overall and by segment)
- Estate processing cycle time (time from death notification to account settlement)
- Estate processing error rate
- Customer/family satisfaction scores
- Beneficiary retention rate (percentage of inherited assets that remain)

Report these metrics monthly to the steering committee and quarterly to executive leadership. Show trends over time. Celebrate improvements. Diagnose problems. Make metrics visible so the organization knows this matters.

Phase Three: Infrastructure and Process Transformation (Months 6-18)

With early wins established and momentum building, you're ready for deeper transformation. This is where you address the operational and technology constraints we identified in Chapters 5 and 6.

Deploy Purpose-Built Infrastructure

As we discussed in Chapter 7, most institutions can't achieve Estate Readiness using their existing core banking and document management systems. These systems weren't designed for estate processing, they lack the workflow orchestration, document storage, and family relationship mapping capabilities that Estate Readiness requires.

Rather than waiting years for core system modernization, deploy purpose-built inheritance infrastructure that integrates with your existing systems. Several emerging platforms provide this infrastructure layer, a digital vault and estate orchestration platform that addresses Planning, Documentation, and Execution pillars without requiring core system replacement.

The infrastructure approach offers several advantages:

- **Speed to value.** Purpose-built infrastructure can be deployed in months, not years. You don't need to wait for core modernization to begin capturing Estate Readiness benefits.
- **Reduced risk.** You're not touching mission-critical core systems. The infrastructure layer sits alongside existing systems, connecting them without replacing them.
- **Leveraged investment.** Infrastructure built specifically for estate processing incorporates best practices, regulatory requirements, and workflow optimization that would take years to develop internally.
- **Integration capability.** Modern infrastructure uses APIs to connect with core banking, document management, CRM, and other systems, creating the unified view that estate processing requires without consolidating underlying platforms.

Redesign Estate Processing Workflows

Technology alone doesn't transform operations. You also need to redesign the workflows that technology enables.

Map your target-state estate processing workflow:

- Single point of intake for all death notifications
- Automated case creation and routing
- Consolidated document management with clear status visibility
- Reduced handoffs between departments
- Proactive family communication at defined milestones
- Exception handling processes for complex situations
- Quality assurance checkpoints to catch errors before they reach families

Compare target-state to current-state. Identify every gap. Develop a sequenced plan to close gaps, starting with highest-impact, lowest-complexity changes.

Involve front-line staff in workflow redesign. They know where the workarounds are, where time is wasted, where errors originate. Their input makes redesigned workflows realistic and their involvement builds commitment to change.

Train and Enable Staff

Process transformation requires behavior change. Staff who have processed estates one way for years need support in adopting new approaches.

Training should address both skills and mindset:

- Technical skills: How to use new systems and follow new processes
- Conversation skills: How to discuss estate preparation with customers naturally
- Mindset shift: Why Estate Readiness matters and how their role contributes

Don't rely on one-time training events. Build ongoing reinforcement through coaching, peer learning, job aids, and performance feedback. Research shows that organizations providing continuous reinforcement see adoption rates 40% higher than those relying on launch-day training alone.

Identify change champions, staff members who embrace the new approach enthusiastically and can help peers adopt. Position them as resources and coaches. Celebrate their successes visibly. Early adopters create social proof that accelerates broader adoption.

Implement Phased Rollout

Avoid the temptation to transform everything at once. Phased implementation reduces risk, enables learning, and builds confidence.

Consider phasing by:

- **Geography:** Start with a region or set of branches, refine the approach, then expand
- **Customer segment:** Begin with high-value customers where the stakes are highest, then broaden
- **Capability:** Implement document storage first, then workflow automation, then advanced analytics

- **Function:** Transform intake processing first, then mid-process documentation, then settlement and transition

Each phase provides learning that improves subsequent phases. Early phases surface problems while scope is contained. Success in early phases builds organizational confidence that later phases will succeed.

Phase Four: Optimization and Embedding (Months 18-36)

Launching new capabilities isn't the same as embedding them in organizational culture. Phase Four focuses on making Estate Readiness permanent, part of how your institution operates, not a temporary initiative.

Measure Outcomes, Not Just Activities

Early metrics focus on activities: How many beneficiary designations did we complete? How many staff did we train? How many customers did we contact?

Mature metrics focus on outcomes: Did processing cycle time actually decrease? Did error rates decline? Did beneficiary retention improve? Are families more satisfied?

Shift your measurement emphasis from activities to outcomes. This focuses attention on what matters, actual improvement in estate processing and customer experience, rather than on checking boxes.

Refine Based on Data

Use outcome data to drive continuous improvement. If processing time improved in some branches but not others, diagnose why. If certain customer segments aren't adopting document pre-collection, understand the barriers. If errors persist in particular process steps, investigate root causes.

Establish regular review cycles where cross-functional teams examine data, identify improvement opportunities, and implement refinements. Continuous improvement should be explicit expectation, not occasional activity.

Integrate with Performance Management

Behavior follows incentives. If relationship managers are measured only on new account acquisition, they won't invest time in beneficiary conversations. If operations staff are measured only on transaction throughput, they won't prioritize estate case quality.

Incorporate estate-related activities and outcomes into performance expectations:

- Include beneficiary designation completion in relationship manager goals
- Add estate processing metrics to operations scorecards
- Factor customer satisfaction scores into branch performance assessments
- Recognize staff who exemplify Estate Readiness behaviors

When estate readiness becomes part of how performance is measured and rewarded, it becomes part of how people work.

Sustain Executive Attention

Transformation initiatives often lose momentum after initial implementation. Executives who championed the launch move on to other priorities. Regular reviews become less frequent. Metrics stop being reported. The organization concludes that Estate Readiness was last year's focus.

Guard against attention decay:

- Keep estate readiness on executive meeting agendas permanently
- Report metrics to the board annually
- Connect estate readiness to other strategic priorities (customer experience, digital transformation, regulatory compliance)
- Refresh the narrative with new data and success stories
- Celebrate multi-year improvements, not just launch milestones

The institutions that sustain transformation are those that treat it as permanent priority rather than temporary project.

The Change Management Imperative

Technology and process changes are necessary but not sufficient. Transformation ultimately happens in the minds and behaviors of people.

Change management, the structured approach to helping people adopt new ways of working, is essential.

Communicate the "Why"

People resist change when they don't understand why it's necessary. They embrace change when they see its purpose and believe in its importance.

Communicate the Estate Readiness vision clearly and repeatedly:

- We're helping customers prepare for life's most difficult moments
- We're serving families with compassion and competence when they need us most
- We're building relationships that span generations
- We're protecting the deposits that fund our institution's future

The "why" isn't just about business results, it's about purpose. Staff who understand that Estate Readiness helps families during vulnerable times will embrace the work differently than staff who see it as just another corporate initiative.

Address Resistance Directly

Resistance to change is natural. People fear the unknown, worry about their competence in new systems, and feel comfortable with familiar routines.

Common sources of resistance to Estate Readiness transformation include:

- "We've always done it this way"
- "I don't have time to add estate conversations to my responsibilities"
- "Talking about death is uncomfortable, customers don't want this"
- "The new system is confusing"
- "This is just another management fad that will pass"

Address resistance with empathy and evidence. Acknowledge that change is hard. Provide support and training. Share data showing that customers appreciate estate conversations when handled thoughtfully. Demonstrate that new systems, once learned, are more efficient than old workarounds. Show sustained commitment that proves this isn't a passing fad.

Build Change Capability

Some organizations transform once and struggle. Others develop the capability to transform repeatedly. The difference is whether transformation builds organizational muscle or exhausts organizational patience.

Build change capability by:

- Debriefing transformation experiences, what worked, what didn't, what you'll do differently next time
- Developing internal change management expertise
- Creating reusable frameworks for future initiatives
- Celebrating adaptability as an organizational value

Estate Readiness transformation is practice for future transformations. The capabilities you build will serve you when the next strategic imperative emerges.

Measuring Transformation Success

How do you know if your transformation is working? Clear metrics, measured consistently, compared against baselines.

Operational Metrics

- Estate processing cycle time (target: 50% reduction from baseline)
- Document requests per case (target: 30% reduction)
- Handoffs per case (target: 50% reduction)
- Processing errors per 100 cases (target: 75% reduction)
- Staff hours per estate case (target: 40% reduction)

Customer Experience Metrics

- Family satisfaction scores (target: top-quartile NPS)
- Complaint rate per 100 estates (target: 50% reduction)
- Time to first proactive family contact (target: <48 hours from notification)
- Percentage of families receiving status updates at defined intervals (target: 100%)

Business Outcome Metrics

- Beneficiary retention rate (target: 15-20 percentage point improvement)
- Retained deposits from inheritance transfers (target: absolute dollar increase)
- New accounts opened by beneficiaries (target: 25% of inherited accounts generate new relationships)
- Customer lifetime value of beneficiaries (target: comparable to acquired customers)

Readiness Metrics

- Beneficiary designation completion rate (target: 80%+ of eligible accounts)
- Document pre-collection rate (target: 25%+ of high-value customers)
- Next-generation engagement rate (target: 20%+ of high-value customers have family members engaged)
- Staff confidence scores on estate conversations (target: 80%+ comfortable)

Establish baselines before transformation begins. Track progress monthly. Report to leadership quarterly. Celebrate improvements. Diagnose and address shortfalls.

The Investment Question

"What will this cost?" is an inevitable question. Here's how to think about it.

Categories of Investment

Estate Readiness transformation requires investment in several categories:

- **Technology:** Purpose-built infrastructure, integration with existing systems, potentially mobile app enhancements for document capture
- **Process redesign:** Staff time to map current state, design target state, document new procedures
- **Training:** Development of training materials, delivery of training programs, ongoing reinforcement

- **Change management:** Communication, resistance management, performance management integration
- **Ongoing operations:** Staff to manage new processes, maintain technology, drive continuous improvement

Building the Business Case

The business case for Estate Readiness rests on three value drivers:

1. **Retention value:** What is the economic value of improving beneficiary retention? If you currently lose 60% of inherited deposits within 12 months, and Estate Readiness reduces that to 40%, what is the value of those retained deposits over their lifetime?
2. **Efficiency value:** What are the operational savings from faster, more accurate estate processing? If you currently spend 8 hours per estate case and Estate Readiness reduces that to 4 hours, what is that time worth across your annual estate volume?
3. **Risk reduction value:** What is the value of reducing errors, complaints, and regulatory issues in estate processing? What are current costs of error correction, complaint resolution, and regulatory response?

For most institutions, the retention value alone justifies the investment. A mid-sized bank processing 500 estates annually with average inherited balances of $150,000 stands to retain an additional $15-20 million in deposits per year with a 20 percentage point improvement in beneficiary retention. Over a three-year horizon, that's $45-60 million in retained deposits, generating ongoing net interest income and creating opportunities for cross-selling.

Return Timeline

Estate Readiness transformation delivers returns over time, not immediately. Expect:

- Months 0-6: Investment exceeds returns as you build foundation
- Months 6-12: Early returns from beneficiary designation improvements and quick wins
- Months 12-24: Growing returns as process transformation takes hold
- Months 24-36: Full returns as capabilities mature and compound

Research from McKinsey suggests that transformation initiatives require 12-24 months for meaningful ROI, with top performers achieving measurable improvements within 18 months. Organizations that try to accelerate this timeline often sacrifice quality for speed, and end up taking longer because they must re-do poorly executed work.

Common Pitfalls and How to Avoid Them

Transformation initiatives fail in predictable ways. Avoid these pitfalls:

Pitfall: Treating it as a technology project

Estate Readiness is a business transformation that uses technology, not a technology implementation with business benefits. When IT owns the initiative, process and culture dimensions get neglected. When the project ends at "go-live," the behavior change that delivers value never happens.

Avoid by: Ensuring business ownership with cross-functional governance. Defining success in business outcome terms, not technology deployment terms. Planning for the 18+ months of behavior change that follow technology implementation.

Pitfall: Underinvesting in change management

Organizations regularly underestimate what it takes to change behavior at scale. They assume that announcing new processes and training on new systems will be sufficient. They're wrong.

Avoid by: Budgeting explicitly for change management. Assigning dedicated resources to communication, training reinforcement, resistance management, and performance integration. Planning for 18-36 months of change management support, not just launch-day training.

Pitfall: Losing executive attention

Executives have many priorities. After the launch announcement, their attention drifts to other matters. Without sustained executive engagement, organizational energy dissipates.

Avoid by: Scheduling regular executive reviews throughout the transformation timeline, not just at launch. Connecting estate readiness to metrics executives care about. Providing executives with data and stories that keep the initiative vivid. Making estate readiness a permanent agenda item, not a one-time topic.

Pitfall: Scope creep

Success breeds ambition. Early wins lead to requests for expanded scope, more customer segments, more product lines, more sophisticated capabilities. Before long, a focused initiative becomes an overwhelming program that can't deliver on any of its promises.

Avoid by: Establishing clear scope boundaries at the outset. Creating governance processes that evaluate scope changes against capacity. Completing Phase One before expanding to Phase Two. Resisting the urge to do everything at once.

Pitfall: Declaring victory too early

Launching new capabilities feels like success. There's temptation to declare victory, disband teams, and move on. But launch is the beginning of transformation, not the end. The hard work of embedding new behaviors and realizing benefits happens after launch.

Avoid by: Defining success in outcome terms (beneficiary retention, processing time) rather than activity terms (system launched, staff trained). Maintaining transformation governance for at least 18 months post-launch. Continuing to measure and report until improvements are sustained and embedded.

Getting Started Tomorrow

Transformation can feel overwhelming. Where do you actually begin?

Here's what you can do in the next 30 days:

1. **Gather data.** Pull numbers on your current estate volume, processing time, beneficiary retention, and designation rates. Ignorance isn't a strategy.
2. **Calculate the stakes.** Estimate the deposits you're losing to poor estate experience. Put a dollar figure on the opportunity.

3. **Identify a sponsor.** Who in your executive team cares about customer experience, deposit retention, or competitive differentiation? Make the case to them.
4. **Map one estate.** Take a recent estate case and map every step from death notification to final settlement. Count the handoffs, the delays, the workarounds. This exercise alone will reveal improvement opportunities.
5. **Talk to families.** Interview 5-10 families who recently experienced estate settlement with your institution. What worked? What frustrated them? What would they change?
6. **Audit designations.** Pull the data on beneficiary designation rates across your customer base. This tells you how ready, or not, you're for estate events today.

These actions require no budget approval, no technology deployment, no organizational restructuring. They require only the decision to begin.

The Urgency of Now

The generational wealth transfer isn't a future event, it's happening now. Every single day, another 10,000 Boomers cross the age 65 threshold. Every year, 2.8 million Americans die, and that number will grow to 3.6 million by 2037. The estates are processing today, the beneficiaries are departing today, the deposits are leaving today.

Institutions that wait to transform will wait too long. By the time they build Estate Readiness capabilities, the peak of the wealth transfer wave will have passed through their customer base, and those customers' assets will have passed to competitors.

The institutions that act now gain compounding advantage. Every month of improved estate processing is a month of better customer experience. Every year of higher beneficiary retention is a year of deposit growth that competitors don't capture. The gap between leaders and laggards widens with time.

Transformation takes 18-36 months to complete. If you start today, you'll have mature Estate Readiness capabilities in 2028 or 2029, in time to capture the peak years of the wealth transfer wave. If you wait another year to start, you'll have mature capabilities in 2029 or 2030, and you'll have lost another year of departed deposits, frustrated families, and competitive disadvantage.

The playbook is here. The opportunity is clear. The question is whether your institution will have the commitment to act.

CHAPTER NINE

The Strategic Imperative

Estate Readiness isn't a standalone initiative. It's not a department project, a technology upgrade, or a customer service enhancement that exists independently of your institution's broader strategy.

Estate Readiness is strategic infrastructure. It connects to, and amplifies, virtually every other priority your institution is pursuing: digital transformation, customer experience, competitive differentiation, deposit growth, relationship deepening, and multigenerational engagement. When executed well, Estate Readiness becomes a force multiplier for institutional strategy.

This chapter explores those connections. It shows how inheritance infrastructure integrates with the initiatives already underway at your institution, and why treating Estate Readiness as a silo is a strategic mistake.

The Convergence Point

Consider the strategic priorities occupying your executive team's attention:

Digital transformation. How do we modernize our technology infrastructure, deliver digital experiences that match customer expectations, and compete with neobanks and fintechs that were born digital?

Customer experience. How do we create seamless, personalized experiences across every touchpoint? How do we build emotional connections that transcend transactional relationships?

Deposit growth and retention. How do we attract and retain deposits in a competitive environment where rates are transparent, switching is easy, and loyalty is fragile?

Relationship deepening. How do we increase share of wallet, cross-sell effectively, and extend customer lifetime value?

Multigenerational engagement. How do we build relationships with younger generations who may not yet be our customers but will inherit our current customers' wealth?

Estate Readiness sits at the convergence of all five priorities. It's a digital capability (requiring modern infrastructure). It's a customer experience differentiator (serving families during life's most difficult moments). It's a deposit retention strategy (keeping inherited wealth with your institution). It's a relationship deepening mechanism (engaging customers in planning conversations). And it's a multigenerational engagement platform (building relationships with beneficiaries before they inherit).

When you see Estate Readiness as the convergence point of your strategic priorities rather than a separate initiative, you unlock synergies that isolated projects can't achieve.

Estate Readiness as Digital Transformation

Most financial institutions are in the midst of digital transformation. They're modernizing core systems, deploying mobile capabilities, automating processes, and leveraging data to personalize customer interactions.

The challenge with digital transformation is focus. There are countless possibilities for digitization. How do you prioritize? Where do you invest?

Estate Readiness offers a compelling answer: invest in digital capabilities that address your most consequential customer interactions.

Death is the ultimate moment of truth. How your institution handles estate settlement shapes family perceptions permanently. A family that has a frustrating, confusing, bureaucratic experience will leave, and tell others. A family served with competence and compassion will stay, and recommend you.

Yet for most institutions, estate processing remains stubbornly analog. Paper documents are faxed between departments. Manual data entry is required at multiple points. Status updates require phone calls. Processing times stretch into months because no one has visibility into the full picture.

This is where digital transformation should begin, not with flashy consumer features but with capabilities that address your institution's most consequential interactions.

Effective inheritance infrastructure represents this kind of consequential digital investment. It provides:

- **Digital document collection and storage.** Customers can upload estate-related documents through secure digital channels, eliminating paper-based processes.
- **Automated workflow orchestration.** Estate cases flow through defined processes with automated routing, status updates, and exception handling.
- **Family communication portals.** Beneficiaries receive proactive status updates through digital channels rather than waiting for callbacks.
- **Integration with existing systems.** Application programming interfaces (APIs) connect inheritance infrastructure to core banking, document management, and customer relationship management (CRM) systems, creating unified views without requiring system replacement.

Digital transformation consultants often recommend starting with "quick wins" that demonstrate value. Estate Readiness is the ultimate quick win for digital transformation: it addresses a real business problem (beneficiary attrition), serves customers during critical moments, and builds digital capabilities that extend to other use cases.

Estate Readiness as Customer Experience

Customer experience has become the primary competitive battleground in financial services. Products are largely commoditized, rates and fees can be compared instantly. Switching costs have declined. What differentiates institutions is how they make customers feel.

Research consistently shows that customer experience drives loyalty, retention, and advocacy. Banks with superior customer experience see 50% higher customer retention rates and 20% greater cross-sell opportunities compared to their peers. In a market where acquiring a new customer costs five to seven times more than retaining an existing one, experience is economics.

Most customer experience programs focus on everyday interactions: mobile app usability, branch wait times, call center responsiveness, digital account opening. These matter. But they're also table stakes, the minimum expectations customers bring from their experiences with Amazon, Netflix, and other digital leaders.

Estate Readiness addresses a different dimension of customer experience: the consequential interaction. How do you serve customers, and their families, during life's most difficult moments?

This is where experience becomes truly differentiating. Anyone can build a decent mobile app. Few institutions excel at estate settlement. The institution that serves families with competence and compassion during grief creates emotional bonds that competitors can't replicate through better rates or shinier technology.

Estate Readiness transforms estate settlement from a pain point into an experience advantage:

- **Proactive communication.** Instead of waiting for confused family members to figure out whom to call, the institution reaches out promptly with clear guidance.
- **Reduced friction.** When documents are pre-collected and beneficiaries are pre-identified, processing happens quickly rather than dragging on for months.
- **Empathetic service.** Staff trained in estate conversations approach families with appropriate sensitivity, not bureaucratic indifference.
- **Transparency.** Families know where things stand without calling repeatedly to ask for updates.

Customer experience programs often struggle to demonstrate ROI because the connections between experience improvements and business outcomes are indirect. Estate Readiness offers direct connections: improved estate experience leads to higher beneficiary retention, which leads to retained deposits, which leads to revenue.

Estate Readiness as Competitive Differentiation

The banking industry faces unprecedented competitive pressure. Neobanks and fintechs offer slick digital experiences. Large national banks leverage scale and technology budgets that regional and community institutions can't match. Differentiation becomes essential for survival.

The conventional differentiation playbook focuses on either price (better rates) or convenience (better technology). Both are problematic strategies. Price-based competition erodes margins. Technology-based competition favors well-capitalized competitors who can outspend you.

Estate Readiness offers a different differentiation path: relationship depth. You compete not on price or features but on the quality of relationships you build, relationships that span life stages, weather difficult moments, and extend across generations.

This is a differentiation that neobanks can't easily replicate. Digital challengers excel at frictionless transactions and attractive interfaces. They struggle with complex, relationship-intensive situations that require human judgment, empathy, and institutional commitment. A neobank can process a peer-to-peer payment instantly. Can it guide a grieving family through estate settlement with competence and care?

Community banks and credit unions have natural advantages here. They know their communities. They employ people who live in those communities. They have branches where families can sit down with someone who understands their situation. Estate Readiness leverages these relational strengths rather than trying to out-tech the tech companies.

The competitive moat created by Estate Readiness is also durable. Technology advantages erode as competitors copy features. Price advantages disappear when competitors match rates. But institutional capability in estate preparation and settlement, built over years through training, process refinement, and accumulated expertise, is difficult to replicate quickly.

An institution known for helping families prepare and for serving them with excellence when death occurs builds a reputation that attracts customers seeking comprehensive financial partners. It becomes the institution families trust for life's most important financial decisions.

Estate Readiness as Deposit Strategy

Deposit gathering and retention remain fundamental to banking economics. Deposits fund loans. Net interest income depends on deposit balances. In an environment of rate competition and easy switching, holding deposits becomes challenging.

Traditional deposit strategies focus on acquisition: attractive rates for new accounts, promotional offers, marketing campaigns. These strategies have their place, but they're expensive and create "hot money" deposits that leave when rates change elsewhere.

Estate Readiness represents a different deposit strategy: retention of inherited wealth. Instead of spending to attract new deposits, you invest in keeping deposits that are already yours, deposits that would otherwise walk out the door when customers die.

The math is compelling. Consider a $3 billion deposit institution with 2,500 customer deaths annually. If the average deceased customer holds $150,000 in deposits, and 60% of inherited wealth departs within 12 months, that's $225 million in annual deposit attrition from estate events alone.

Improving beneficiary retention by 20 percentage points, from 40% retention to 60% retention, would retain an additional $75 million annually. Over five years, that's $375 million in retained deposits, generating ongoing net interest income and creating opportunities for relationship expansion.

Compare this to acquisition costs. If your institution spends $300-500 per acquired deposit relationship and each new relationship brings an average of $15,000 in deposits, retaining $75 million through Estate Readiness is equivalent to acquiring 5,000 new relationships, at a fraction of the cost.

Estate Readiness also addresses deposit quality. Inherited deposits often represent concentrated wealth from customers who banked with your institution for decades. These are stable, relationship-based deposits rather than rate-sensitive promotional deposits. Retaining them strengthens your funding base.

Estate Readiness as Relationship Deepening

Financial institutions often speak of "relationship deepening" increasing the products, services, and engagement that each customer has with the institution. Deeper relationships generate more revenue, increase retention, and extend customer lifetime value.

Research suggests that increasing customer retention by just 5% can increase profits by 25% to 95%. After one purchase, a customer might return a quarter of the time. After two purchases, the likelihood nearly doubles. After three, it reaches roughly 62%. Each additional product strengthens the relationship.

Traditional relationship deepening focuses on cross-selling: moving customers from checking to savings, from deposits to loans, from banking to wealth management. These strategies work, but they often feel transactional to customers, another product push from their bank.

Estate Readiness offers relationship deepening that feels like care rather than selling. When you help customers prepare for wealth transfer, you're not pushing products, you're addressing their genuine concerns about family wellbeing, legacy protection, and life planning.

Consider what Estate Readiness conversations involve:

- Reviewing beneficiary designations to ensure they reflect current wishes
- Discussing family relationships and how wealth should transfer
- Storing important documents securely so families can access them when needed
- Introducing adult children to the institution so relationships span generations
- Connecting customers with estate planning resources and professionals

Each of these interactions deepens the customer relationship. Each creates data that informs future engagement. Each makes the customer more connected to your institution and less likely to leave for a competitor offering marginally better rates.

Estate orchestration technology facilitates this deepening by providing a reason for ongoing engagement. The digital vault gives customers a place to store and update documents. Life event triggers prompt beneficiary reviews.

Family mapping identifies opportunities for next-generation outreach. The platform becomes a relationship infrastructure, not just a processing system.

Estate Readiness as Multigenerational Strategy

The great wealth transfer will move $84 trillion through 2045. The beneficiaries receiving this wealth are, in many cases, completely unknown to the institutions holding their parents' and grandparents' assets.

This is the generational gap in banking. Institutions have deep relationships with older customers who hold the majority of deposits. They have shallow or nonexistent relationships with the younger generations who will inherit those deposits. When wealth transfers, relationships don't automatically transfer with it.

Research from wealth management firms shows that 89% of high-net-worth advisory firms now cite family-focused services as a top growth strategy. They've learned through painful experience that failing to engage heirs before inheritance leads to mass asset departures afterward.

Banks and credit unions face the same dynamic. The next generation banks somewhere: often not with their parents' institution. They have no particular loyalty to an institution they've never used. When they inherit, they consolidate to their existing bank, not the one holding the inherited accounts.

Estate Readiness breaks this pattern by engaging multiple generations during the customer's lifetime:

- **Family meetings.** Invite customers to bring adult children to conversations about estate planning and family financial management.
- **Beneficiary awareness.** When beneficiaries are designated, ensure they know they've been named and understand what will happen when they eventually inherit.
- **Youth accounts and family linkages.** Encourage customers to open accounts for children and grandchildren, creating relationships that can grow into primary banking relationships.
- **Financial education.** Offer programs for younger generations that provide genuine value while introducing them to your institution.

These touchpoints build familiarity before inheritance. When beneficiaries inherit into an institution they already know, where they've met staff, attended programs, perhaps opened their own accounts, retention improves dramatically.

Effective inheritance infrastructure supports multigenerational engagement by mapping family relationships and tracking beneficiary information. It identifies opportunities for next-generation outreach. It provides a reason for family conversations that would otherwise feel awkward to initiate.

Multigenerational strategy isn't a separate initiative from Estate Readiness, it's an integral component. You can't engage the next generation without talking about wealth transfer. You can't prepare for wealth transfer without engaging the next generation.

The Trust Advantage

Throughout this discussion, one theme recurs: trust.

Customers trust your institution with their money. Estate Readiness invites them to trust you with something more, their wishes, their family information, their planning for moments when they won't be present to advocate for themselves.

This deeper trust creates competitive advantage that transcends features and rates:

- A customer who has stored estate documents with your institution has made a commitment that's difficult to unwind
- A customer who has introduced family members has expanded the relationship beyond themselves
- A customer who has documented wishes and preferences has invested time and emotional energy in the relationship

Each dimension of trust increases switching costs, not contractual switching costs, but emotional and practical ones. The customer who has built Estate Readiness with your institution would have to rebuild it elsewhere to leave.

This is the defensive moat that Estate Readiness creates. While competitors can match your rates tomorrow, they can't replicate the trust relationships you've built with customers and their families over years.

Trust also extends across generations. When beneficiaries inherit into an institution that has handled their family's affairs with competence and care, they inherit trust along with assets. They've seen your institution at its best, serving their family during a difficult time. That experience becomes the foundation of their own relationship with you.

Integration, Not Isolation

The strategic power of Estate Readiness emerges only when it's integrated with broader institutional strategy rather than siloed as a specialty function.

Integration with digital transformation. Inheritance infrastructure should be part of your digital roadmap, not a separate track. The APIs, workflows, and data capabilities you build for Estate Readiness extend to other use cases. The digital document management you implement for estate preparation serves document-intensive processes throughout the institution.

Integration with customer experience. Estate Readiness training should align with broader customer experience programs. The empathy, communication skills, and relationship orientation required for estate conversations enhance every customer interaction. Customer experience metrics should include estate-related measures.

Integration with deposit strategy. Estate Readiness should be part of how you think about deposit retention, not a separate initiative. Report beneficiary retention alongside other retention metrics. Include estate-related deposits in deposit forecasting. Factor Estate Readiness into deposit pricing and competitive positioning.

Integration with relationship management. Estate Readiness conversations should be part of relationship manager routines, not occasional events. Beneficiary reviews should be triggered by life events alongside other account reviews. Family relationships should be captured in CRM alongside individual customer data.

Integration with marketing. Estate Readiness capabilities should be part of how you position your institution in the market. When families are choosing a financial partner for comprehensive service, Estate Readiness differentiates. Marketing messaging should reflect this capability.

The institutions that treat Estate Readiness as an isolated department or project will capture only a fraction of its potential value. The institutions that integrate it throughout their strategy will find it amplifying every other initiative they pursue.

The Fintech Threat and the Trust Response

The competitive landscape in banking continues to evolve. Neobanks and fintechs have captured meaningful market share, particularly among younger customers, with slick digital experiences, low fees, and innovative features.

These challengers are formidable in transactional banking. They excel at payments, basic accounts, and digital interfaces. They've proven that customers will switch for superior digital experience.

But they face significant challenges in relationship-intensive domains:

- Neobanks lack branch networks for complex conversations
- They lack institutional history and stability that reassures customers during major decisions
- They lack the workforce to provide personalized guidance during difficult situations
- They lack the trust that comes from decades of community presence

Estate Readiness plays to traditional institutions' strengths while fintechs face structural disadvantages. A neobank can process a death notification, but can it guide a grieving family through estate settlement with the human touch that moments require? Can it conduct family conversations about wealth transfer? Can it build multigenerational relationships through community presence?

This isn't an argument for complacency. Traditional institutions must continue improving digital capabilities. But it's an argument for strategic clarity: compete where you have advantages, not where challengers have advantages.

Estate Readiness is a domain where traditional institutions, particularly community banks and credit unions, can compete from strength. Local presence, relationship depth, institutional stability, and human-centered service are assets in estate preparation and settlement. Leverage them.

From Defense to Offense

Throughout this book, we've discussed Estate Readiness partly in defensive terms: stopping deposit attrition, retaining inherited wealth, preventing beneficiary departure. These defensive benefits are real and substantial.

But Estate Readiness also creates offensive opportunities:

Customer acquisition. Customers seeking comprehensive financial partners, particularly those with complex family situations or significant wealth, will be attracted to an institution known for estate preparation and settlement. Estate Readiness becomes a differentiated value proposition that draws customers who might otherwise choose based on rates alone.

Wealth management expansion. Estate Readiness conversations naturally connect to wealth management services. Customers preparing for wealth transfer often need investment management, trust services, and financial planning. These conversations become lead generation for higher-margin services.

Advisory fee revenue. Some institutions offer fee-based estate planning coordination services. The expertise developed through Estate Readiness enables revenue-generating advisory offerings that go beyond traditional banking.

Referral generation. Families served well during estate settlement become advocates. They recommend your institution to friends, colleagues, and extended family. Word-of-mouth from families who experienced exceptional estate service is powerful marketing.

Community positioning. An institution known for helping families prepare and serving them during difficult times builds community reputation that extends beyond individual relationships. It becomes the institution that "takes care of families" a positioning that attracts customers across life stages.

Estate Readiness isn't just about stopping losses. It's about creating value, for customers, families, communities, and the institution itself.

The Time Horizon

Strategic initiatives require patience. Estate Readiness is no exception.

The full benefits of Estate Readiness compound over time:

- Year 1-2: Foundation building. Infrastructure deployment. Staff training. Early customer conversations. Initial beneficiary designation improvements.
- Year 2-4: Process maturation. Workflow optimization. Growing document pre-collection rates. Expanding next-generation engagement. Measurable improvements in estate processing metrics.
- Year 4-7: Relationship depth. Customers who prepared years ago experience estate events. Families served well become advocates. Institutional reputation builds. Competitive differentiation becomes visible.
- Year 7-10: Generational impact. Multiple generations of relationships. Sustained deposit retention. Market positioning as the institution for multigenerational wealth.

Institutions seeking quick returns will be disappointed. Estate Readiness requires investment before returns materialize. Customers must prepare before they die. Families must experience excellent service before they recommend. Reputation must build before it attracts.

But institutions with strategic patience will be rewarded. The relationships built today become the retained deposits of tomorrow. The beneficiaries engaged today become the customers of the decade ahead. The trust established today becomes the competitive moat of the generation to come.

The great wealth transfer is a 20-year phenomenon. Institutions thinking on 20-year horizons will capture disproportionate value.

Strategic Questions for Your Institution

As you consider how Estate Readiness connects to your institutional strategy, reflect on these questions:

Digital transformation alignment:

- How does estate processing fit in your digital transformation roadmap?

- Are you investing in digital capabilities for your most consequential customer interactions?
- Does your digital strategy address multigenerational engagement?

Customer experience integration:

- Do you measure customer experience during estate settlement?
- Are staff trained to handle estate conversations with appropriate empathy?
- Is estate experience part of how you think about customer journey mapping?

Competitive positioning:

- How do you differentiate from neobanks and fintechs?
- Are you competing on your strengths (relationships, trust, human service) or their strengths (digital slickness, low fees)?
- What would it mean to be known in your market as the institution for multigenerational wealth?

Deposit strategy:

- Do you track beneficiary retention as a deposit metric?
- How much deposit attrition results from estate events annually?
- What would improving beneficiary retention by 15-20 percentage points mean for your deposit base?

Relationship deepening:

- Are beneficiary conversations part of relationship manager routines?
- Do you capture family relationship data alongside individual customer data?
- How do you engage the next generation before inheritance?

The answers to these questions reveal whether your institution is positioned to capture the Estate Readiness opportunity, or positioned to watch competitors capture it instead.

The Choice

We return to where this book began: the demographic wave that can't be stopped.

The wave continues: 10,000 Boomers reaching 65 every day. Every year, 2.8 million Americans die, rising to 3.6 million by 2037. Cerulli projects $84 trillion transferring through 2045.

The wealth transfer will happen whether your institution is ready or not. The question is whether you'll capture value from it, or watch that value flow to competitors.

Estate Readiness isn't just an operational improvement or a customer service enhancement. It's strategic infrastructure for the demographic transition that will reshape banking over the next two decades. It connects to every priority your institution is pursuing. It leverages strengths that your most dangerous competitors can't match. It builds competitive advantages that compound over time.

The institutions that recognize this strategic imperative, and act on it, will thrive. They'll retain deposits that competitors lose. They'll build relationships that span generations. They'll establish reputations that attract customers seeking partners, not just providers.

The institutions that don't will watch wealth walk out the door. They'll wonder why their deposit base is shrinking. They'll struggle to explain why the next generation banks elsewhere. They'll lose ground in a competition they didn't realize they were in.

The strategic imperative is clear. The direction you choose will define your institution for the next two decades.

CHAPTER TEN

The Economics of Estate Readiness

Strategy requires investment. Investment requires justification. Justification requires numbers.

This chapter provides those numbers. It translates the strategic arguments of previous chapters into financial terms that CFOs understand, boards approve, and institutions can track over time. We'll build a comprehensive business case for Estate Readiness, quantify the sources of value, calculate return on investment, and address the objections skeptics raise.

The economics of Estate Readiness are compelling, more compelling than most technology investments financial institutions evaluate. But they require a different lens than traditional ROI analysis. The returns compound over time. The benefits span multiple dimensions. The baseline costs are often hidden in existing operations. Understanding the full picture requires structured analysis.

Let's build that picture.

The Three Value Drivers

Estate Readiness generates value through three distinct mechanisms. A complete business case must quantify all three.

Value Driver 1: Deposit Retention

This is the primary value driver. When customers die, their deposits are at risk. Beneficiaries inherit assets but not relationships. Without intervention, the majority of inherited wealth leaves the institution within 12 months.

Estate Readiness reverses this dynamic. By preparing customers during their lifetimes, engaging beneficiaries before inheritance, and delivering excellent estate settlement experience, institutions retain deposits that would otherwise depart.

The math is straightforward:

Deposit Retention Value = Annual Deaths × Average Deposit Balance × Retention Rate Improvement × Value per Retained Dollar

Let's work through an example:

Variable	Your Institution	Example
Annual customer deaths	________	2,500
Avg deposit balance at death	$________	$150,000
Current retention rate	________%	40%
Target retention rate	________%	60%
Net interest margin	________%	2.5%
Current hours per estate	________	8 hours
Target hours per estate	________	4 hours
Fully loaded labor cost/hr	$________	$45

- Annual savings: 2,500 × 4 hours × $45 = $450,000

This $450,000 in annual savings represents approximately 2.2 FTEs of recovered capacity. That capacity can be redeployed to higher-value activities or absorbed as headcount grows more slowly than estate volume.

Additionally, consider error reduction. Estate processing errors require correction, often consuming more time than the original task. They generate complaints, occasionally create legal exposure, and damage family relationships. If Estate Readiness reduces error rates by 50%, the additional savings in rework and complaint resolution could add another $100,000-$150,000 annually.

Value Driver 3: Relationship Expansion

Estate Readiness creates opportunities for relationship expansion that wouldn't otherwise exist:

- **Cross-sell during preparation.** Customers preparing for wealth transfer often need wealth management services, trust services, or insurance products. Estate Readiness conversations become natural entry points for these higher-margin offerings.

- **New relationship acquisition.** Beneficiaries who stay become full customers, not just inherited account holders. They open additional accounts, consolidate assets from other institutions, and engage with your full product set.
- **Referral generation.** Families served well during estate settlement recommend your institution to others. Word-of-mouth from a positive estate experience carries exceptional credibility.

Quantifying relationship expansion is more speculative than retention or efficiency, but conservative estimates are valuable:

Relationship Expansion Value = New Products per Retained Beneficiary × Revenue per Product × Number of Retained Beneficiaries

If Estate Readiness retains an additional 500 beneficiary relationships annually (20% of 2,500 deaths), and each retained beneficiary eventually adds 1.5 products beyond the inherited accounts, generating $200 per product in annual revenue:

- Additional revenue from relationship expansion: 500 × 1.5 × $200 = $150,000 annually

This figure grows as relationships mature. A beneficiary retained at age 45 has decades of potential relationship value. The customer lifetime value of a retained beneficiary, considering all products, services, and referrals over a 20-30 year relationship, could exceed $5,000-$10,000.

Building the Business Case

With the three value drivers quantified, we can assemble a comprehensive business case. Together, they translate the threat of generational wealth transfer into a language every CFO and board member understands: return on investment. This is how you take estate orchestration from a conversation to a commitment.

Annual Value Generation

Value Driver	Annual Value
Deposit Retention (NII)	$1,875,000
Operational Efficiency	$450,000
Error Reduction	$125,000
Relationship Expansion	$150,000
Total Annual Value	**$2,600,000**

Investment Requirements

Estate Readiness requires investment in several categories:

Technology Infrastructure

- Inheritance infrastructure platform licensing: $150,000-$300,000 annually (varies by institution size)
- Integration with existing systems: $75,000-$150,000 (one-time)
- Ongoing technical support: $25,000-$50,000 annually

Process Redesign

- Current-state mapping and analysis: $50,000-$75,000 (one-time)
- Target-state workflow design: $50,000-$75,000 (one-time)
- Process documentation and training materials: $25,000-$50,000 (one-time)

Training and Change Management

- Staff training program development: $50,000-$75,000 (one-time)
- Training delivery (relationship managers, operations staff): $75,000-$100,000 (one-time)
- Ongoing training for new staff: $25,000-$50,000 annually

Program Management

- Transformation project management: $100,000-$150,000 (Year 1)

- Ongoing program management: $50,000-$75,000 annually (Years 2+)

Investment Summary

Category	Year 1	Year 2	Year 3	Year 4	Year 5
Technology (ongoing)	$200K	$200K	$200K	$200K	$200K
Technology (one-time)	$125K				
Process Redesign	$175K				
Training (one-time)	$175K				
Training (ongoing)	$25K	$35K	$35K	$35K	$35K
Program Management	$150K	$75K	$75K	$75K	$75K
Total Investment	**$850K**	**$310K**	**$310K**	**$310K**	**$310K**

Value Realization Timeline

Value doesn't materialize immediately. The phased implementation described in Chapter 8 means benefits accrue gradually:

- Year 1: Foundation building. Limited value realization, perhaps 20% of steady-state value
- Year 2: Process maturation. Growing value, perhaps 50% of steady-state value
- Year 3: Full capability. Near steady-state value, perhaps 85% of steady-state value
- Year 4+: Optimization. Full steady-state value plus compound benefits

Year	Value Realized	Investment	Net Value
Year 1	$520,000 (20%)	$850,000	($330,000)
Year 2	$1,300,000 (50%)	$310,000	$990,000
Year 3	$2,210,000 (85%)	$310,000	$1,900,000
Year 4	$2,600,000 (100%)	$310,000	$2,290,000
Year 5	$2,600,000 (100%)	$310,000	$2,290,000
5-Year Total	**$9,230,000**	**$2,090,000**	**$7,140,000**

Return on Investment

Five-year ROI = Net Value / Total Investment = $7,140,000 / $2,090,000 = 342%

Payback period: Approximately 18 months (break-even occurs early in Year 2)

These returns significantly exceed typical technology investment hurdles. Most institutions require 15-25% annual ROI for technology projects. Estate Readiness delivers returns well above that threshold.

Sensitivity Analysis

Business cases rest on assumptions. Responsible analysis tests those assumptions through sensitivity analysis.

Conservative Scenario

What if retention improvement is only 10 percentage points instead of 20? What if processing efficiency improves 25% instead of 50%? What if relationship expansion benefits are negligible?

Value Driver	Conservative Estimate
Deposit Retention	$937,500
Operational Efficiency	$225,000
Error Reduction	$75,000
Relationship Expansion	$50,000
Total Annual Value	**$1,287,500**

Even with these conservative assumptions, five-year net value exceeds $3 million, and ROI remains above 150%. The payback period extends to approximately 28 months but still delivers compelling returns.

Optimistic Scenario

What if retention improvement reaches 25 percentage points? What if processing efficiency improves 60%? What if relationship expansion benefits are substantial?

Value Driver	Optimistic Estimate
Deposit Retention	$2,343,750
Operational Efficiency	$540,000
Error Reduction	$175,000
Relationship Expansion	$300,000
Total Annual Value	**$3,358,750**

Five-year net value approaches $12 million, ROI exceeds 500%, and payback occurs within 15 months.

Key Sensitivity Variables

The business case is most sensitive to:

1. **Retention rate improvement.** This is the largest value driver. Each percentage point of additional retention improvement adds approximately $95,000 in annual net interest income.
2. **Average deposit balance at death.** Institutions serving wealthier customers see proportionally larger retention benefits. If average balance is $250,000 instead of $150,000, the retention value driver increases by 67%.
3. **Net interest margin.** Higher margins increase the value of retained deposits. A 3.0% margin instead of 2.5% increases retention value by 20%.
4. **Estate volume.** Larger institutions with more customer deaths see proportionally larger benefits, with relatively similar investment requirements, creating economies of scale.

The Hidden Costs You're Already Paying

One objection to Estate Readiness investment is "we can't afford it." This objection ignores the costs you're already incurring, the costs of not being ready.

Deposit Attrition Costs

Your institution loses deposits every time a customer dies and beneficiaries depart. This attrition has real economic impact.

If your institution processes 2,500 deaths annually with average balances of $150,000 and loses 60% of inherited deposits within 12 months, you're losing $225 million in deposits annually. At a 2.5% net interest margin, that's $5.6 million in annual net interest income, walking out the door every year.

You're already paying this cost. You're just not tracking it.

Processing Inefficiency Costs

Your staff spend thousands of hours annually on estate processing, much of it inefficient. The 8 hours per case documented in Chapter 5 includes significant waste: chasing documents, re-entering data, checking status, correcting errors.

At 2,500 cases and 8 hours per case, your institution devotes 20,000 hours annually to estate processing, approximately ten full-time employees' worth of capacity scattered across departments. Much of this time produces no value for families or the institution.

You're already paying this cost. You're just not optimizing it.

Customer Experience Costs

Poor estate experience drives families away, not just from the inherited accounts but from their own accounts with your institution. When a son watches his mother struggle with your institution's estate process, he moves his own accounts too.

The ripple effects of poor estate experience extend beyond direct beneficiaries to extended family, friends who hear about the experience, and community reputation. These costs are real but difficult to quantify.

Competitive Vulnerability Costs

Institutions that don't invest in Estate Readiness create competitive openings for institutions that do. As the market for multigenerational wealth services matures, institutions known for estate excellence will attract customers seeking comprehensive financial partners.

The cost of competitive vulnerability is the customers you never acquire because you didn't have the capabilities they sought.

Comparing to Alternative Investments

Capital is scarce. Every dollar invested in Estate Readiness is a dollar not invested elsewhere. How does Estate Readiness compare to alternative uses of funds?

Branch Renovation

Many institutions invest $1-2 million per branch in renovations. These investments improve customer experience and may attract new customers, but ROI is difficult to measure and often disappointing.

Estate Readiness investment of $850,000 in Year 1 delivers measurable returns that compound over time. The payback is faster and the ROI is clearer than most branch renovation projects.

Digital Banking Enhancement

Digital banking improvements compete for the same technology dollars as Estate Readiness. But digital enhancements often deliver incremental improvements to everyday interactions, while Estate Readiness transforms consequential interactions.

A mobile app feature that saves customers 30 seconds per session is valuable. A transformation that retains $75 million in deposits annually is transformational. Both matter, but the scale of impact differs substantially.

Customer Acquisition Campaigns

Marketing campaigns to acquire new customers typically cost $300-500 per acquired relationship. If each new relationship brings $15,000 in average deposits, your cost to acquire $75 million in new deposits would be $1.5-2.5 million annually.

Estate Readiness achieves the same deposit impact, $75 million retained, for approximately $310,000 in ongoing annual investment (after Year 1). Retention is dramatically more cost-effective than acquisition.

Loan Growth Initiatives

Loan growth is valuable, but loans require funding. Retained deposits provide that funding. Estate Readiness supports loan growth by stabilizing and expanding your deposit base.

The Compound Effect

Simple ROI calculations understate Estate Readiness value because they don't capture compounding.

Deposit Compounding

Each year, you retain additional deposits that would otherwise have departed. These deposits remain on your books, generating net interest income year after year.

Year	New Deposits Retained	Cumulative Retained	Annual NII
1	$75,000,000	$75,000,000	$1,875,000
2	$75,000,000	$150,000,000	$3,750,000
3	$75,000,000	$225,000,000	$5,625,000
4	$75,000,000	$300,000,000	$7,500,000
5	$75,000,000	$375,000,000	$9,375,000

By Year 5, cumulative retained deposits reach $375 million, generating $9.4 million in annual net interest income. This compound effect dramatically exceeds the simple annual value calculation.

(Note: This simplified model assumes deposits remain indefinitely. In practice, some retained deposits will attrit over time. A more sophisticated model would apply deposit decay rates. Even with decay assumptions, the compound effect remains substantial.)

Relationship Compounding

Retained beneficiaries don't just hold inherited accounts, they expand relationships over time. The beneficiary retained at age 45 who adds a mortgage, investment account, and business banking relationship over the following 20 years generates lifetime value far exceeding the initial inherited deposit.

Reputation Compounding

Each family served well becomes an advocate. Their recommendations attract new customers who, in turn, become advocates themselves. The reputation effect compounds as positive experiences accumulate and spread through community networks.

Capability Compounding

The capabilities you build for Estate Readiness extend to other use cases. Document management infrastructure serves other document-intensive processes. Workflow automation patterns apply to other complex workflows. Staff trained in difficult conversations handle other sensitive situations more effectively.

Addressing Objections

Every business case faces skeptical questions. Here are the most common objections to Estate Readiness investment and how to address them:

"We can't measure beneficiary retention, so we can't prove the value."

This objection reveals a data gap, not a business case flaw. If you can't measure beneficiary retention, you should measure it, regardless of whether you invest in Estate Readiness. Understanding your current state is essential to managing the business.

Start by tracking a cohort of estates. Measure deposit balances at death and at 6, 12, and 24 months post-death. Calculate the percentage retained. This baseline enables ROI measurement and reveals the scale of your current attrition problem.

"Our beneficiaries leave because of rates, not experience."

Some beneficiaries leave for rates. But research consistently shows that experience, not rates, drives the majority of banking relationship decisions. Families who have a positive estate experience are far more likely to consolidate assets with your institution than to chase marginal rate advantages elsewhere.

Moreover, Estate Readiness addresses rate competition indirectly. Beneficiaries with existing relationships (developed through next-generation engagement) are less likely to comparison shop. Beneficiaries who trust your institution (based on estate experience) value that trust over basis points.

"We don't have the budget."

Every institution has budget constraints. The question is priorities, not absolute dollars. If Estate Readiness delivers 342% ROI over five years, it should rank highly among competing priorities.

Consider phased investment. Start with beneficiary designation campaigns and customer conversation pilots, low-cost interventions that build the case for larger investment. Use early wins to justify infrastructure investment.

Also consider opportunity cost. The $5.6 million in annual net interest income lost to deposit attrition is a "cost" you're paying today. Estate Readiness investment reduces that cost.

"Technology implementations always cost more and deliver less than projected."

This skepticism is warranted, many technology projects disappoint. Mitigate implementation risk through:

- Phased rollout that validates assumptions before full deployment
- Clear success metrics established before implementation begins
- Vendor partnerships with implementation expertise
- Executive sponsorship that maintains attention through the full implementation cycle

Purpose-built inheritance infrastructure reduces implementation risk compared to custom development or enterprise system configuration. The platform is designed for estate processing, not adapted from general-purpose systems.

"We don't have the organizational capacity for another transformation initiative."

Transformation fatigue is real. Institutions can only absorb so much change simultaneously.

However, Estate Readiness can be scoped to match organizational capacity. A focused initiative targeting beneficiary designations and customer conversations requires minimal technology change. A comprehensive transformation with full infrastructure deployment demands more capacity.

Match scope to capacity. Start where you are. Build momentum before expanding.

Making the Case to Your Board

Board presentations require different emphasis than operational analysis. Directors want strategic rationale, risk assessment, and clear accountability.

Strategic Rationale

Frame Estate Readiness as demographic response. The board has likely seen data on aging customers and wealth transfer. Connect Estate Readiness to that macro context:

"Our average customer age is 58 and rising. Over the next 15 years, a substantial portion of our deposit base will transfer to the next generation. Estate Readiness ensures we retain those deposits rather than losing them to competitors."

Risk Assessment

Address both implementation risk and the risk of inaction:

Implementation risks: Technology deployment challenges, staff adoption rates, customer response uncertainty. Mitigated through phased implementation, change management investment, and pilot programs.

Inaction risks: Accelerating deposit attrition, competitive disadvantage, failure to serve aging customers appropriately. These risks compound with every year of delay.

Accountability

Boards want to know who's responsible and how success will be measured:

"The Chief Retail Officer will sponsor this initiative with direct reports from Operations and Technology. We will measure success through beneficiary retention rate, estate processing cycle time, and family satisfaction scores. Quarterly progress reports will come to the board."

The Ask

Be specific about what you need:

"We're requesting approval of an $850,000 Year 1 investment to establish Estate Readiness capabilities, with projected ongoing investment of $310,000 annually. Based on conservative projections, this investment will generate positive ROI within 18 months and deliver $7 million in net value over five years."

Tracking and Reporting

Investment requires accountability. Establish metrics from Day One and report consistently.

Leading Indicators (measure monthly during implementation)

- Beneficiary designation completion rate (target: increase by 15 percentage points in Year 1)
- Estate conversation volume (target: establish baseline, then grow 20% quarterly)
- Document pre-collection rate (target: establish baseline, then grow 25% quarterly)
- Staff training completion (target: 100% of relevant staff within 6 months)
- System deployment milestones (target: on-schedule delivery per implementation plan)

Lagging Indicators (measure quarterly, track trends)

- Estate processing cycle time (target: 40% reduction by end of Year 2)

- Estate processing error rate (target: 50% reduction by end of Year 2)
- Beneficiary retention rate (target: 15-20 percentage point improvement by end of Year 3)
- Family satisfaction scores (target: top-quartile NPS by end of Year 2)
- Net interest income from retained deposits (target: track against projections)

Financial Reporting

Report Estate Readiness value in familiar financial terms:

- Deposits retained (quarterly tracking against attrition baseline)
- Net interest income from retained deposits (monthly calculation)
- Processing cost savings (quarterly estimation)
- Investment vs. budget (standard project tracking)
- Cumulative ROI vs. projection (quarterly update to leadership)

The Long-Term View

Estate Readiness economics improve over time. The first year is investment-heavy with limited returns. Years 2-3 see growing returns as capabilities mature. Years 4+ deliver full value with compound effects.

Institutions that take a long-term view, investing patiently, measuring consistently, and optimizing continuously, will capture maximum value from Estate Readiness.

The institutions that demand immediate payback or abandon initiatives before maturity will capture only a fraction of potential value.

The great wealth transfer is a 20-year phenomenon. Institutions thinking in 20-year horizons will build Estate Readiness capabilities that compound over decades, not months.

Estate Readiness Financial Model Template

Use this template to build your institution-specific business case:

Input Variables

Annual customer deaths __________ 2,500

Average deposit balance at death $__________ $150,000

Current beneficiary retention rate __________% 40%

Target retention rate with Estate Readiness __________% 60%

Net interest margin on deposits __________% 2.5%

Current processing hours per estate __________ 8 hours

Target processing hours with Estate Readiness __________ 4 hours

Fully loaded labor cost per hour $__________ $45

Value Driver Calculations

Deposit Retention Value

Retention improvement: _________% (Target - Current)

Deposits retained through improvement: ________ deaths × $________ avg balance × % improvement = $______ annually

Net interest income from retained deposits: $__________ × % NIM = $______ annually

Operational Efficiency Value

Hours saved per case: ________ (Current - Target)

Annual labor savings: ________ deaths × ________ hours saved × $________ per hour = $__________ annually

Total Annual Value

Deposit retention NII + Operational efficiency + Error reduction (estimate) + Relationship expansion (estimate) = $__________

Investment and ROI

Category	Your Estimate
Year 1 total investment	$________
Annual ongoing investment (Years 2+)	$________
Annual steady-state value	$________
Payback period	________ months
5-year ROI	________%

CHAPTER ELEVEN

The Human Dimension

Technology can automate workflows. It can store documents, trigger notifications, route cases, and generate reports. It can even analyze patterns and predict behaviors with remarkable accuracy.

But technology can't hold a widow's hand while she signs papers through tears. It can't read the tension between siblings who haven't spoken in years. It can't sense when a grieving son needs silence rather than information. It can't recognize that this family needs more time, while that family needs swift resolution.

No two families are the same. Every death brings a unique constellation of relationships, emotions, histories, and needs. The institution that recognizes this, that builds human capacity to meet families where they are, one family at a time, will create an advantage that no algorithm can replicate.

This chapter is about the human dimension of Estate Readiness: the people who make it work, the skills they need, and the culture that sustains them. In an era when everyone is racing toward automation and artificial intelligence, the institutions that preserve and invest in human capability will find themselves with something increasingly rare and valuable, genuine connection at life's most difficult moments.

The Automation Paradox

Every financial institution is pursuing automation. The rationale is sound: reduce costs, increase consistency, accelerate processing, scale operations without proportional headcount growth. AI-powered chatbots handle routine inquiries. Workflow engines route cases without human intervention. Document recognition extracts data automatically. The efficiency gains are real.

But there's a paradox embedded in this pursuit: as routine interactions become automated, the remaining human interactions become more important, not less.

When a customer calls about a balance inquiry, automation serves them well. When a customer calls because their father just died and they don't know what to do, automation fails them catastrophically.

The first interaction is transactional. The second is consequential. And as institutions automate more transactional interactions, the consequential interactions represent an ever-larger share of what humans actually do. This concentrates emotional intensity. It raises the stakes of each human touchpoint. It demands more from the people who remain.

Estate Readiness sits squarely in consequential territory. These aren't routine transactions. These are families navigating loss, confusion, legal complexity, and financial uncertainty, often simultaneously. They need humans who can meet them with competence and compassion. They need institutions that have invested in building that capability.

The institutions that recognize this paradox will invest in human capacity even as they invest in automation. They'll understand that technology and humanity aren't competing priorities, they're complementary ones. Technology handles the routine so humans can focus on the consequential. Technology provides information so humans can provide judgment. Technology ensures consistency so humans can provide personalization.

The institutions that don't recognize this paradox will automate their way into irrelevance. They'll build efficient systems that families hate. They'll process estates quickly but lose beneficiaries permanently. They'll optimize metrics while destroying relationships.

What Families Actually Need

To build human capacity for Estate Readiness, we must first understand what families actually need when death occurs.

They need to be seen. Grieving families don't want to be case numbers. They want to be recognized as people experiencing something difficult. The staff member who says, "I'm so sorry about your mother. How are you holding up?" before launching into paperwork requirements creates a different experience than the one who says, "I need your case number."

They need clarity in confusion. Death creates administrative chaos. Families don't know what to do, whom to call, or what documents they need. They need patient explanation, often repeated explanation, because grief impairs concentration and memory. They need someone willing to answer the same question three times without frustration.

They need pace that matches their emotional state. Some families want to move quickly through estate matters, action provides a sense of control. Others need more time, they're not ready to close accounts that bear their parent's name. Human judgment recognizes these differences. Systems don't.

They need navigation, not just information. Information about estate settlement is available everywhere. What families need is someone who can navigate them through their specific situation. "Here's what typically happens" is less valuable than "Here's what I recommend for your situation, given what you've told me."

They need to feel that someone cares. This seems obvious, but it's often absent in institutional interactions. Staff members under time pressure, following scripts, processing cases, can come across as indifferent even when they're not. Families remember how they were treated. They remember whether anyone seemed to care.

They need consistent relationships, not handoffs. Being transferred between departments, re-explaining the situation to each new person, and receiving conflicting information from different staff members compounds family stress. Whenever possible, families benefit from a consistent point of contact who knows their situation.

These needs can't be fully met by technology. They require human presence, human judgment, and human connection. The institution that develops people capable of meeting these needs will create experiences that families remember, and return for.

The Skills That Matter

What skills distinguish staff members who serve families well during estate settlement from those who struggle? Through observation of exceptional estate service, consistent patterns emerge.

Emotional Intelligence

Emotional intelligence, the ability to recognize, understand, and respond appropriately to emotions in oneself and others, is foundational. Staff members with high emotional intelligence:

- Read family emotional states accurately
- Adjust their communication style to match what families need
- Maintain composure when families express frustration or grief
- Recognize when to provide information versus when to provide presence
- Sense dynamics between family members that aren't explicitly stated

Emotional intelligence isn't a fixed trait. Research shows that structured training can improve emotional intelligence, with studies showing effect sizes of 0.44-0.58 from targeted interventions. Institutions that invest in emotional intelligence development see measurable improvements in customer satisfaction, often 15-25% gains in satisfaction scores.

Active Listening

Active listening goes beyond hearing words. It involves full attention, acknowledgment, and response that demonstrates understanding. Staff members skilled in active listening:

- Give families their complete attention, without distraction
- Acknowledge emotions before addressing logistics
- Reflect back what they've heard to confirm understanding
- Ask follow-up questions that show genuine engagement
- Allow silence when silence is needed

In estate conversations, active listening serves multiple purposes. It builds trust. It surfaces information that families might not volunteer unprompted. It makes families feel valued rather than processed.

Difficult Conversation Navigation

Estate settlement inevitably involves difficult conversations: explaining why certain documents are required, discussing timelines that may not meet family expectations, addressing disputes between beneficiaries, delivering news that families don't want to hear.

Staff members who navigate difficult conversations well:

- Prepare for conversations rather than improvising
- Frame difficult information with empathy before delivery
- Use "yes, and" rather than "no, because" framing whenever possible
- Offer alternatives when requests can't be fulfilled
- Know when to escalate versus when to handle themselves

The ability to have difficult conversations without damaging relationships is rare and valuable. It can be developed through training, practice, and feedback.

Technical Competence

Empathy without competence frustrates families as much as competence without empathy. Staff members need deep understanding of:

- Account types and their transfer mechanics
- Beneficiary designation rules and requirements
- Documentation requirements for different situations
- Regulatory constraints and timelines
- Internal processes and escalation paths

Technical competence enables confidence. Staff members who know their domain thoroughly can answer questions without hesitation, anticipate complications before they arise, and navigate unusual situations without constant supervisory consultation.

Judgment Under Ambiguity

Estate situations rarely follow neat patterns. Families present situations not covered by policy. Documents are incomplete. Relationships are unclear. Timelines conflict with family needs.

Staff members with good judgment:

- Know when to apply rules strictly versus when to seek exceptions
- Escalate appropriately, neither too readily nor too reluctantly
- Make reasonable assumptions when information is incomplete
- Balance family needs with institutional requirements
- Document decisions clearly for future reference

Judgment develops through experience, coaching, and exposure to diverse situations. Institutions that give staff members authority to exercise judgment, within appropriate boundaries, develop this capacity faster than those that demand rigid adherence to scripts.

Building the Team

Estate Readiness requires a team with differentiated roles. Not everyone needs every skill to the same degree. Effective teams combine specialists whose capabilities complement each other.

Estate Services Specialists

These are the backbone of estate operations, staff members who process estate cases day to day. They need:

- Strong technical competence in estate procedures
- Emotional intelligence sufficient for routine family interactions
- Efficiency in case management
- Attention to detail in documentation
- Ability to recognize when cases require escalation

Estate Services Specialists handle the volume. They ensure cases move through the system properly. They're the first point of contact for many families.

Family Relationship Managers

For complex estates, high-value relationships, or situations requiring elevated sensitivity, Family Relationship Managers provide dedicated support. They need:

- Exceptional emotional intelligence

- Deep expertise in estate complexities
- Strong judgment for ambiguous situations
- Communication skills for difficult conversations
- Relationship-building orientation

Family Relationship Managers handle fewer cases but handle them more deeply. They're assigned to the estates that matter most, either because of relationship value or because of situation complexity.

Estate Readiness Advisors

Before death occurs, Estate Readiness Advisors conduct the preparation conversations, beneficiary reviews, document collection, family introductions. They need:

- Consultative conversation skills
- Knowledge spanning estate planning, beneficiary designations, and document requirements
- Comfort initiating conversations about sensitive topics
- Relationship-building orientation across generations
- Ability to coordinate with relationship managers and product specialists

Estate Readiness Advisors operate upstream, reducing estate complexity before it occurs. Their work makes Estate Services Specialists' work easier.

Team Leadership

Estate team leaders need management capabilities specific to emotionally demanding work:

- Recognition of compassion fatigue and stress in team members
- Ability to debrief difficult cases supportively
- Coaching skills for developing emotional intelligence and judgment
- Workflow management to balance caseloads appropriately
- Connection to broader institutional strategy

Leadership sets the tone. Teams led by managers who model empathy and prioritize family experience perform differently than teams led by managers who prioritize efficiency metrics alone.

Training That Transforms

Generic customer service training doesn't prepare staff for estate conversations. The emotional stakes are higher. The complexity is greater. The consequences of poor handling are more severe.

Effective estate readiness training addresses specific competencies through methods that build real capability.

Foundation Training: The Human Experience of Loss

Before technical training, your staff needs to understand what families experience. Foundation training covers:

- The grief process and its variation across individuals
- How grief affects cognition, communication, and decision-making
- Cultural differences in grief expression and death rituals
- The administrative burden families face during bereavement
- Common family dynamics during estate settlement

This foundation builds empathy. Staff members who understand what families are experiencing approach them differently than those who see only cases to process.

Technical Training: Estate Mechanics

Technical training ensures that your staff knows what they're doing:

- Account types and transfer requirements
- Beneficiary designation mechanics
- Documentation requirements by situation type
- Regulatory framework and compliance requirements
- Internal systems and processes

Technical training can be delivered through e-learning, classroom instruction, and hands-on practice. Mastery requires all three.

Skill Training: Conversations That Connect

The most transformative training develops conversation skills through practice:

- Role-playing difficult scenarios with feedback

- Practicing emotional acknowledgment and validation
- Developing language for common challenging situations
- Learning when to speak and when to listen
- Building comfort with silence

Role-playing is essential. Reading about empathetic communication doesn't build the skill. Practicing it, with coaches who provide real-time feedback, does.

Hospice organizations, which specialize in supporting families through death and grief, typically provide 20-30 hours of initial training for bereavement volunteers, including education about grief, communication skills development, and extensive role-playing. Financial institutions serving families during estate settlement face similar challenges and need similar preparation.

Scenario-Based Learning

Real capability develops through exposure to realistic scenarios:

- The grieving widow who can't find any documents
- The siblings who disagree about everything
- The beneficiary who wants everything done yesterday
- The family member who suspects fraud
- The estate with legal complications

Each scenario type presents different challenges. Staff members who have practiced these scenarios, thought through responses, received feedback, refined their approach, handle real situations more effectively.

Ongoing Development

Initial training isn't sufficient. Skills erode without reinforcement. New situations arise. Best practices evolve. Ongoing development includes:

- Regular team discussions of challenging cases
- Periodic role-play refreshers
- Updates on regulatory changes
- Sharing of successful approaches across the team

- Individual coaching for staff members facing specific development needs

Research shows that continuous reinforcement leads to 40% higher adoption of desired behaviors than one-time training alone.

The Culture That Sustains

Individual skills matter, but culture determines whether those skills are applied consistently. Culture shapes what people actually do when no one is watching. It determines whether family-first behavior is rewarded or merely tolerated.

Leadership Modeling

Culture flows from leadership. When leaders demonstrate genuine concern for families, when they celebrate team members who go above expectations, when they personally handle escalated cases with empathy, they set standards that cascade through the organization.

Leaders who focus exclusively on efficiency metrics without balancing them against experience metrics signal that families are secondary. Staff members notice. They adjust their behavior accordingly.

Permission to Care

Many staff members want to serve families well but feel constrained by time pressure, performance metrics, or uncertainty about boundaries. Effective cultures give explicit permission to care:

- "Take the time you need with families"
- "Use your judgment, we trust you"
- "It's okay to stay on the phone until they feel supported"
- "I'd rather you spent extra time with one family than rushed through three"

Permission matters. Staff members who feel empowered to provide exceptional service will. Those who feel constrained to process cases efficiently will do that instead.

Recognition and Reward

What gets recognized gets repeated. Cultures that celebrate staff members who deliver exceptional family experience, through formal recognition, storytelling, performance evaluations, and advancement decisions, develop more people who deliver exceptional experience.

Conversely, cultures that only recognize productivity metrics develop people who optimize for productivity. This isn't wrong, efficiency matters, but it's incomplete.

Psychological Safety

Estate work is emotionally demanding. Staff members who engage deeply with grieving families absorb emotional weight. Cultures that support staff wellbeing sustain performance over time:

- Regular check-ins on how staff members are doing emotionally
- Permission to step away after particularly difficult cases
- Debriefing opportunities for processing challenging situations
- Recognition that compassion fatigue is real and must be managed
- Access to support resources when needed

Research on hospice workers, who face similar emotional demands, shows that compassion fatigue creates cynicism and emotional exhaustion when not addressed. Staff members suffering from compassion fatigue become less effective, regardless of their inherent capability.

Continuous Improvement Orientation

Cultures that get better over time embrace learning from every interaction:

- After-action reviews of challenging cases
- Systematic capture of what works and what doesn't
- Openness to feedback from families
- Willingness to change processes that aren't working
- Humility about current capabilities

The institution that learns fastest wins. This applies to estate readiness as much as any other domain.

AI as Enabler, Not Replacement

The rise of artificial intelligence in banking raises inevitable questions: Will AI replace the human dimension of estate service? Should institutions invest in human capability when technology is advancing so rapidly?

The answer is nuanced. AI can enable better human service. It can't replace it.

Where AI Adds Value

AI excels at tasks that benefit from speed, consistency, and pattern recognition:

- Document classification and data extraction
- Case routing to appropriate teams
- Status updates and routine notifications
- Compliance checking and exception flagging
- Predictive identification of at-risk cases
- Knowledge retrieval for complex regulatory questions

These capabilities free human capacity for higher-value activities. They ensure routine matters are handled consistently while humans focus on situations requiring judgment and empathy.

AI can also support human interactions directly:

- Prompting staff with relevant information about family situations
- Suggesting next-best-actions based on case characteristics
- Providing real-time guidance during complex conversations
- Identifying sentiment signals in communications
- Enabling continuous personalization across touchpoints

Research shows that 80% of routine banking tasks can be automated through AI. But estate settlement isn't routine. The 20% that can't be automated, the consequential interactions, represent the majority of value creation.

Where AI Falls Short

AI can't replicate:

- Genuine emotional connection with grieving families
- Judgment about when rules should bend
- Recognition of family dynamics that aren't explicitly stated
- The pause that acknowledges a family needs a moment
- The tone that communicates care beyond words
- The relationship that builds trust over time

A recent study found that 72% of banking customers would consider returning to banks that provide more human-like, empathetic interactions, suggesting that even as AI improves, the demand for human connection persists.

The Human-AI Partnership

The most effective approach combines AI capability with human capacity:

- AI handles document processing; humans handle family emotions
- AI routes cases efficiently; humans exercise judgment about exceptions
- AI provides information instantly; humans provide interpretation and guidance
- AI ensures nothing falls through cracks; humans ensure families feel cared for
- AI scales capacity; humans provide personalization

Banks like Huntington are showing how this partnership works. They use AI to personalize communications and surface insights while training branch and contact center staff to translate those insights into meaningful human connections. The goal isn't automation for its own sake, it's practical support that helps customers while maintaining the human touch.

The institution that sees AI as a human enabler rather than a human replacement will build capability that compounds. AI gets better at its tasks. Humans, freed from routine work, get better at theirs. The combination delivers experiences that neither could achieve alone.

Personalization at Scale

The fundamental challenge of Estate Readiness is personalization at scale. You can't afford to assign a dedicated relationship manager to every estate. But you also can't serve families well with one-size-fits-all processes. The solution lies in structured personalization, systems and practices that enable tailored service without requiring custom handling for every case.

Segmentation

Not every estate requires the same level of attention. Effective segmentation directs resources appropriately:

- **Relationship value:** Higher-value customers warrant more intensive support
- **Estate complexity:** Multi-account, multi-beneficiary situations need more attention
- **Family dynamics:** Situations with conflict or special circumstances require elevated care
- **Beneficiary opportunity:** Estates where retention is particularly valuable or at-risk merit extra investment

Segmentation enables tiered service. Simple estates can be handled efficiently. Complex estates receive the attention they need. Resources flow to where they create most value.

Structured Flexibility

Processes can provide structure while enabling flexibility:

- Core steps that every estate follows
- Decision points where staff exercise judgment
- Escalation paths for situations outside normal parameters
- Documentation that captures context for future interactions
- Timeframes that can flex based on family needs

Structure without flexibility creates rigidity that families resent. Flexibility without structure creates inconsistency that undermines quality. The combination enables personalization at scale.

Technology-Enabled Personalization

Technology can support personalization even in routine interactions:

- CRM data that provides context for every family contact
- Communication templates that personalize automatically
- Workflow rules that adapt based on case characteristics
- Document portals that reflect family-specific status
- Notification preferences that honor family choices

When staff have relevant information at their fingertips, they can personalize without extensive research. When systems adapt to family characteristics, even automated communications feel tailored.

Human Judgment as the Final Filter

Ultimately, personalization requires human judgment. Technology can suggest; humans must decide:

- "This family needs more time. I'm extending their deadline"
- "This beneficiary is upset. I'm assigning them to our most experienced specialist"
- "This situation is unusual. I'm escalating for guidance"
- "This family appreciates directness. I'll get straight to the point"
- "This family needs hand-holding. I'll walk through every step"

Building staff capacity to exercise this judgment, and trusting them to do so, is the key to personalization at scale.

The Competitive Advantage

In an industry racing toward automation, human capability becomes differentiating.

When every institution has AI-powered chatbots, document extraction, and workflow automation, those technologies become table stakes. They're necessary for efficiency but insufficient for differentiation. Everyone has them. No one wins on them alone.

What differentiates is what technology can't replicate: the staff member who recognizes that this family needs something different. The conversation that makes a widow feel genuinely cared for. The judgment that bends rules appropriately. The relationship that spans generations.

This is the competitive advantage of human capability in Estate Readiness:

It's difficult to copy. Technology can be licensed or built. Culture, capability, and institutional commitment to human service can't be acquired overnight. They develop over years through intentional investment.

It creates emotional connections. Families who experience exceptional human service form bonds with the institution. These bonds persist through rate changes, competitive offers, and switching costs. They create loyalty that transcends transactions.

It generates advocacy. When families are served exceptionally during difficult moments, they tell others. Word-of-mouth from estate experience carries credibility that advertising can't match.

It compounds over time. Staff members get better with experience. Culture strengthens with reinforcement. Reputation builds with accumulated positive experiences. The advantage grows rather than erodes.

It aligns with demographic reality. The customers who hold most of your deposits are aging. The interactions that matter most to them, estate preparation, estate settlement, are inherently human. Serving them well requires human capability.

The institution that sees human capability as a competitive advantage, and invests accordingly, will separate from competitors who see it as a cost to minimize.

From Transaction Processors to Trusted Companions

The transformation Estate Readiness requires is ultimately a transformation of role. Staff members must shift from processing transactions to accompanying families through difficult passages.

This shift parallels a concept from bereavement care called "companioning." Developed by grief educator Dr. Alan Wolfelt, companioning distinguishes between treating people (fixing problems, moving them through stages) and accompanying them (being present, honoring their experience, walking alongside).

In banking terms:

Transaction processing is getting the paperwork done, the accounts transferred, the case closed. It's measuring cycle time and efficiency ratios. It's treating estates as problems to solve.

Companioning is being present to families during difficulty. It's honoring their experience, their grief, their confusion, their individual needs. It's walking alongside them until they're ready to continue. It's treating estates as passages to navigate.

Both matter. Paperwork must get done. But the institution that treats families as problems to process will be resented. The institution that accompanies families through difficulty will be remembered.

This shift requires:

- Reframing the role from processing to accompanying
- Training different skills including emotional presence and active listening
- Measuring different outcomes including family experience and satisfaction
- Structuring work differently to allow time for genuine connection
- Recognizing different behaviors that demonstrate care rather than speed

It's a profound shift. But it's the shift that separates exceptional estate service from adequate estate processing.

Starting the Human Transformation

Building human capability for Estate Readiness doesn't require massive upfront investment. It requires intentional, sustained focus. Here's how to begin:

Month 1-3: Assess Current Capability

- Interview staff about their experiences with estate cases
- Observe estate interactions (with permission) to understand current approach
- Survey families who've been through recent estate settlement
- Identify staff members who naturally excel at estate service
- Document gaps between current capability and ideal capability

Month 4-6: Develop the Training Foundation

- Create foundation training on grief and family experience
- Update technical training to reflect current estate processes
- Develop role-play scenarios for common estate situations
- Identify training resources (internal expertise, external programs)
- Train a cohort of pilot participants

Month 7-9: Pilot and Refine

- Deploy trained staff on estate cases
- Gather feedback from staff and families
- Refine training based on what works and what doesn't
- Develop coaching protocols for ongoing development
- Create measurement framework for human capability

Month 10-12: Scale and Sustain

- Expand training to broader staff population
- Implement ongoing development programs
- Embed human capability into performance management
- Establish team leadership practices that sustain culture
- Integrate human capability with technology investments

Year 2 and Beyond: Deepen and Differentiate

- Advanced training for high-complexity situations
- Specialization development for family relationship managers
- Culture reinforcement through recognition and storytelling

- Continuous improvement based on family feedback
- Integration of human capability into institutional brand

The timeline is flexible. The principle isn't: building human capability requires sustained commitment, not one-time training.

The Choice Before You

As you consider Estate Readiness, you face a choice about the human dimension.

One path prioritizes efficiency. It invests heavily in automation, seeking to minimize human involvement in estate processing. It views labor as a cost and technology as a solution. It measures cycle time and throughput. It may achieve operational efficiency while losing family connection.

Another path prioritizes relationships. It invests in human capability alongside technology, recognizing that both are essential. It views labor as an asset and technology as an enabler. It measures family experience alongside operational metrics. It may sacrifice some efficiency while gaining lasting connection.

The institutions that will thrive through the great wealth transfer are those that choose relationships, that recognize no two families are the same, that build human capacity for personalization at scale, that create experiences families remember and return for.

Technology is necessary. Everyone will have it. Human capability is differentiating. Few will build it.

That difference, the difference between institutions that process estates efficiently and institutions that accompany families through difficulty, will determine which institutions retain inherited wealth and which watch it walk away.

The direction you choose will define your institution for the next two decades.

Human Capability Assessment

Use this framework to evaluate your institution's current human capability for Estate Readiness:

Staff Skills Assessment

Skill Area	Current Level(1-5)	Development Priority(H/M/L)
Emotional intelligence	_____	_____
Active listening	_____	_____
Difficult conversation navigation	_____	_____
Technical competence (estate processes)	_____	_____
Judgment under ambiguity	_____	_____
Family relationship building	_____	_____

Training Program Assessment

Element	In Place?	Quality (1-5)
Foundation training on grief/family experience	Y / N	_____
Technical training on estate processes	Y / N	_____
Role-play and scenario practice	Y / N	_____
Ongoing skill reinforcement	Y / N	_____
Coaching for individual development	Y / N	_____

Culture Assessment

Indicator	Agree (1-5)
Leadership models empathy and family-first behavior	_____
Staff feel empowered to exercise judgment for families	_____
Recognition rewards exceptional family service	_____

Psychological safety supports staff wellbeing _____

Continuous improvement orientation is evident _____

Overall Human Capability Readiness

Based on the assessments above, rate your institution's human capability for Estate Readiness:

☐ Not Ready: Significant gaps in skills, training, and culture

☐ Foundation Building: Some elements in place, Development needed

☐ Developing: Solid foundation with room for improvement

☐ Strong: Well-developed capability across most dimensions

☐ Industry Leading: Exceptional capability that differentiates in market

CHAPTER TWELVE

The Future of Inheritance

The great wealth transfer isn't a moment. It's a movement, a 25-year transformation that will reshape banking, wealth management, and the relationship between families and financial institutions.

We stand at the beginning, not the middle. The demographic wave is just cresting. The generational wealth transfer stretches to 2048 and beyond. The institutions that build Estate Readiness capabilities today aren't responding to a crisis, they're positioning for a generation.

This concluding chapter looks forward. It examines the forces that will shape inheritance infrastructure over the coming decades: demographic evolution, technological innovation, regulatory change, and shifting family dynamics. It considers what institutions must do not just to survive the transition, but to lead it.

The future belongs to those who prepare.

The Demographic Trajectory

The demographics are settled. Actuarial tables don't change quickly. The population of Americans over 65 will grow from 58 million today to 82 million by 2040 and 95 million by 2060. Annual deaths will rise from 2.8 million to 3.6 million by 2037 and continue climbing.

This isn't speculation. These people have already been born. They're aging predictably. Their wealth is accumulating. Their mortality is certain.

What remains uncertain is how this demographic trajectory will intersect with other forces:

Longevity extension. Medical advances continue extending lifespans. The fastest-growing demographic segment is people over 85. Longer lives mean longer wealth accumulation, larger eventual estates, and extended periods of estate preparation. But they also mean more complex end-of-life situations, cognitive decline, extended care needs, and family dynamics that span four or even five generations.

Wealth concentration. The wealth transfer isn't distributed evenly. Approximately $62 trillion, half the total, will come from the top 2% of households. High-net-worth and ultra-high-net-worth families face estate complexities that average families don't: multi-jurisdictional assets, family business succession, philanthropic structures, and tax optimization strategies. Institutions serving these families need sophisticated estate capabilities.

Intergenerational complexity. Wealth won't flow directly from Baby Boomers to grandchildren. Significant transfers will first pass "sideways" to surviving spouses, an estimated $54 trillion to spouses before subsequent intergenerational transfer. An estimated $40 trillion will pass to widowed women, reshaping who controls wealth. By 2030, women will control $34 trillion in investable assets, triple what they held at the start of this decade.

Generational character. The recipients of inherited wealth bring different attitudes than their parents:

- Gen X, receiving $39 trillion, approaches finances pragmatically after losing 38% of their net worth in the 2008 crisis
- Millennials, receiving $46 trillion, favor digital engagement, values-based investing, and self-directed financial management
- Gen Z, expecting significant inheritance, exhibits higher risk tolerance and interest in alternative assets including cryptocurrency

These generational differences demand different engagement strategies, communication channels, and service models.

The Technological Frontier

Technology will transform estate preparation and settlement. The question isn't whether but how, and who will lead the transformation.

Artificial Intelligence

AI will reshape estate operations across multiple dimensions:

Document intelligence. AI-powered document recognition will extract information from estate documents automatically, death certificates, wills, trust documents, beneficiary designations, reducing manual data entry and accelerating processing.

Predictive analytics. Machine learning models will identify at-risk estates earlier: customers showing signs of cognitive decline, families with unresolved beneficiary designations, and estates likely to face complications. Early identification enables proactive intervention.

Conversational AI. Natural language interfaces will handle routine estate inquiries: status updates, document requirements, and timeline questions. AI will triage complex situations to human specialists while managing routine interactions at scale.

Decision support. AI will assist staff with complex judgment calls: suggesting escalation paths, identifying similar past cases, and recommending exception handling based on institutional precedent.

AI won't replace the human dimension of estate service. It will augment it, handling routine matters so humans can focus on consequential interactions, providing information so humans can provide judgment.

Blockchain and Smart Contracts

Blockchain technology offers transformative potential for inheritance:

Immutable records. Blockchain creates tamper-proof records of beneficiary designations, estate documents, and ownership transfers. Once recorded, documents can't be altered without leaving a permanent trail.

Smart contract execution. Self-executing contracts can automate certain inheritance transfers when conditions are verified: releasing cryptocurrency wallets to designated beneficiaries upon confirmed death, distributing assets according to pre-programmed instructions.

Digital asset inheritance. As more wealth exists in digital form, cryptocurrencies, NFTs, digital accounts, blockchain-based inheritance solutions become essential. Traditional estate mechanisms weren't designed for assets that exist only as private keys.

Reduced intermediation. Smart contracts potentially bypass some traditional estate intermediaries: executing transfers automatically rather than waiting for court orders, distributing assets without executor involvement for qualifying situations.

The regulatory and legal frameworks for blockchain-based inheritance are still evolving. Not all jurisdictions recognize smart contracts as binding estate documents. But the technology's potential is clear, and early adoption will create competitive advantage.

Digital Vaults and Secure Storage

Estate Readiness depends on document availability. Digital vault technology will become standard infrastructure for estate-ready institutions:

Centralized document storage. Families store wills, trusts, beneficiary designations, account information, and personal instructions in secure digital repositories. When death occurs, authorized parties can access everything needed.

Life event triggers. Intelligent systems detect life events, death registrations, incapacity determinations, and initiate appropriate workflows automatically.

Family coordination. Shared access enables family members to collaborate on estate preparation while maintaining appropriate access controls.

Integration with institutions. Digital vaults integrate with financial institutions, transmitting documents and information directly rather than requiring manual transfer.

The institutions that integrate with, or provide, digital vault infrastructure will have advantages in estate processing efficiency and customer engagement.

Biometric Authentication and Identity

Estate settlement requires identity verification across multiple parties: confirming death, authenticating beneficiaries, validating document signers. Biometric technology offers more secure and efficient verification:

Voice and facial recognition for remote identity verification Liveness detection to prevent fraud in digital verification Continuous authentication throughout estate processes Integration with government identity systems for death verification

As remote estate settlement becomes more common, robust identity verification becomes essential.

The Regulatory Evolution

Estate settlement sits at the intersection of multiple regulatory domains: banking, securities, insurance, tax, and probate law. Regulatory change in any domain affects estate operations.

Probate Modernization

Probate systems in most jurisdictions remain paper-based, court-centric, and slow. Reform pressure is building:

Simplified small estate procedures. States are raising thresholds for simplified probate. California, for example, now allows a simplified petition for primary residences up to $750,000. Higher thresholds mean more estates can bypass traditional probate.

Electronic filing and records. Courts are slowly digitizing probate processes: electronic filing, digital records, remote hearings. Digital transformation in the courts will eventually streamline estate settlement.

Uniform laws adoption. The Uniform Probate Code and similar model laws continue spreading, creating more consistency across states. Consistency simplifies multi-jurisdictional estates.

Progress is uneven. Some jurisdictions move faster than others. But the direction is clear: gradual modernization that eventually streamlines estate processing.

Banking Regulation

Banking regulators increasingly recognize the importance of estate-related customer protection:

Nomination expansion. India's Banking Laws (Amendment) Act 2025 now allows depositors to appoint up to four nominees, reducing succession disputes. Similar expansions may emerge in other jurisdictions.

Beneficiary designation requirements. Regulators may eventually require institutions to ensure beneficiary designations are complete and current, treating incomplete designations as customer protection issues.

Death notification procedures. Standardized procedures for death notification and account handling may emerge, creating more consistency across institutions.

Digital asset regulation. As digital assets become more common, regulatory frameworks for their treatment in estates will develop. Institutions holding digital assets will need clear procedures for estate situations.

Regulatory change creates both compliance burden and competitive opportunity. Institutions that lead on estate customer protection may earn regulatory goodwill.

Tax Policy

Estate tax policy shapes wealth transfer behavior:

Federal estate tax exemption. The current $13.99 million exemption is scheduled to drop to approximately $7 million in 2026 absent legislative action. Lower exemptions would affect more families and increase estate planning complexity.

State estate and inheritance taxes. State-level taxes vary widely and continue evolving. Multi-state families face particular complexity.

Retirement account rules. The SECURE Act eliminated stretch IRAs, requiring most inherited retirement accounts to be distributed within 10 years. This accelerates wealth transfer timelines.

Tax policy changes create planning windows. Institutions that help customers navigate tax transitions add value beyond basic banking services.

Shifting Family Structures

The families receiving inherited wealth differ from previous generations:

Smaller families. Fertility rates have declined across developed economies. Smaller families mean fewer heirs per estate, but also fewer family members to share caregiving responsibilities and estate administration burdens.

Blended families. Divorce, remarriage, and blended families create complex inheritance situations. Stepchildren, half-siblings, and multiple marriage assets complicate beneficiary designations and create potential for disputes.

Geographic dispersion. Families are more geographically dispersed than ever. Adult children may live across the country or around the world from aging parents. Remote estate administration becomes necessary.

Delayed life milestones. Millennials and Gen Z are marrying later, having children later, and buying homes later than previous generations. These delays affect when inherited wealth arrives in the life cycle and how it's used.

Diverse family structures. Non-traditional families, unmarried partners, LGBTQ+ families, chosen family networks, may not fit traditional inheritance frameworks. Institutions serving diverse families need flexible approaches.

These structural changes demand estate infrastructure that accommodates complexity rather than assuming traditional family patterns.

What Winners Will Do

In this evolving landscape, which institutions will thrive? The winners will share common characteristics:

They Will Start Early

The institutions building Estate Readiness capabilities now will have mature capabilities when the demographic wave peaks. Those waiting until estate volumes force action will scramble to catch up.

Starting early means:

- Building infrastructure before capacity is constrained
- Training staff before volume overwhelms them
- Establishing customer relationships before death occurs
- Creating competitive reputation before the market crowds

The compound effects of early action are substantial. Each year of head start accumulates advantage.

They Will Integrate Across Generations

Winners won't treat estate settlement as an end-of-life service. They'll integrate estate preparation throughout the customer lifecycle:

- Young adult account opening includes beneficiary education
- Life event milestones trigger beneficiary reviews
- Mid-career conversations include estate planning
- Retirement planning connects to wealth transfer strategy
- Active engagement continues through end of life

This lifecycle integration creates multiple touchpoints, builds deeper relationships, and ensures estate readiness when the time comes.

They Will Serve the Whole Family

Winners will build relationships with multiple generations simultaneously:

- Primary customers (wealth holders)
- Spouses and partners (potential first inheritors)
- Adult children (likely beneficiaries)
- Grandchildren (eventual beneficiaries)

Multi-generational relationships create retention that single-generation relationships can't match. When the primary customer dies, the institution already has relationships with inheritors.

They Will Blend Technology and Humanity

Winners won't choose between technology and human service. They'll combine both:

- Technology for efficiency, consistency, and scale
- Humans for empathy, judgment, and connection
- AI to surface insights and handle routine
- People to provide personalization and care

The optimal blend will evolve as technology improves, but the principle remains: consequential interactions require human presence even as routine interactions become automated.

They Will Measure What Matters

Winners will track estate-related metrics systematically:

- Beneficiary designation completion rates
- Estate processing cycle time
- Beneficiary retention rates
- Family satisfaction scores
- Multi-generational relationship depth
- Staff capability assessments

What gets measured gets managed. Institutions that track estate performance will improve faster than those that don't.

They Will Build Distinctive Culture

Winners will cultivate cultures that prioritize families during difficult moments:

- Leadership modeling of empathy and care
- Staff empowerment to exercise judgment
- Recognition of exceptional family service
- Investment in skill development
- Protection against compassion fatigue

Culture is difficult to copy. Institutions with strong estate service cultures will maintain advantages that technology alone can't provide.

The Competitive Landscape Ahead

The competitive landscape for inheritance infrastructure will evolve significantly:

Fintech Disruption

Fintech companies are already entering estate-adjacent spaces:

- Digital will and trust platforms
- Beneficiary management services
- Estate administration software

- Family communication tools
- Digital asset inheritance solutions

These entrants lack banking licenses and customer relationships. But they bring fresh perspectives, modern technology, and user experiences unburdened by legacy systems. Traditional institutions that don't modernize estate services will face competitive pressure from these new entrants.

Wealth Management Convergence

The line between banking and wealth management continues blurring. Wealth management firms have long understood that estate transitions are critical retention moments. Their family-focused practices, multigenerational engagement strategies, and sophisticated estate planning capabilities provide models that banks can learn from.

Conversely, banks' branch networks, deposit relationships, and community presence offer advantages that wealth managers lack. The institutions that combine banking strengths with wealth management sophistication will be well-positioned.

Big Tech Ambitions

Large technology companies continue expanding into financial services. Google, Apple, and Amazon all have payment and financial products. Should they enter estate-related services, they would bring massive technology capability, enormous customer bases, and proven digital experience design.

Traditional institutions can't match big tech's technology resources. But they can compete on trust, relationship depth, and human service, dimensions where big tech has less advantage.

Industry Consolidation

Smaller institutions may lack the resources to build comprehensive estate infrastructure. This could accelerate consolidation, with larger institutions acquiring smaller ones partly for their customer relationships. Alternatively, shared infrastructure through banking associations or fintech partnerships could enable smaller institutions to offer sophisticated estate services without building everything themselves.

The Institution You Must Become

Throughout this book, we've examined the challenge, the opportunity, and the path forward. Now we arrive at the fundamental question: What kind of institution must you become to thrive through the great wealth transfer?

You must become an institution that sees families, not just customers.

Individual customer relationships are insufficient for the demographic transition ahead. You must see families: the aging wealth holder, the surviving spouse, the adult children, the grandchildren. You must build relationships with all of them, understand their dynamics, and prepare for the transitions that will inevitably come.

You must become an institution that prepares, not just processes.

Processing estates after death is necessary but insufficient. You must prepare customers for wealth transfer while they're alive: ensuring beneficiary designations are current, collecting critical documents, introducing family members, having conversations that matter. Preparation transforms estate settlement from crisis management to planned transition.

You must become an institution that companions families through difficulty.

Efficiency in estate processing matters, but it's not enough. You must be present with families during grief, confusion, and transition. You must provide human connection alongside administrative competence. You must be remembered for how you made families feel, not just how quickly you processed paperwork.

You must become an institution that spans generations.

Your oldest customers are approaching the end of their lives. Your youngest customers are just beginning theirs. You must build capabilities that serve both, and everyone in between. You must think in decades, not quarters. You must build relationships that outlast any individual customer.

You must become an institution that integrates technology with humanity.

Technology will transform estate operations. AI, blockchain, digital vaults, and biometrics will change what's possible. But technology alone can't serve grieving families. You must blend technological capability with human capacity, using each where it adds most value. The institutions that get this blend right will lead.

You must become an institution that earns trust.

Trust is the foundation of everything. Customers must trust you with their wealth, their wishes, their family information. Families must trust you during their most vulnerable moments. Future generations must trust that you'll serve them as well as you served their parents and grandparents. Trust is earned through consistent action over time. It can't be bought or shortcut.

The 20-Year Horizon

The great wealth transfer stretches to 2048 and beyond. That's a 20+ year horizon, longer than most planning cycles, longer than most careers, longer than some institutions survive.

Thinking on this horizon requires:

Patient investment. Returns from Estate Readiness compound over time. Year 1 investments don't fully pay off until Year 5 or Year 10. Leadership must sustain commitment through the building period, trusting that foundations laid today enable capabilities tomorrow.

Adaptive strategy. The landscape will change in ways we can't predict. Technology will evolve. Regulations will shift. Customer expectations will rise. Family structures will change. Strategy must adapt while maintaining consistent direction toward multigenerational relationship excellence.

Generational leadership. The executives who launch Estate Readiness initiatives may retire before full benefits materialize. Leadership transitions must preserve strategic commitment. The institutions that sustain focus across leadership generations will capture more value than those that restart with each new CEO.

Cultural reinforcement. Culture erodes without reinforcement. The values, practices, and priorities that distinguish exceptional estate service must be continuously cultivated, through hiring, training, recognition, and daily leadership examples.

A Call to Action

You've read this book. You understand the demographic imperative. You've seen the opportunity and the path forward. Now comes the moment of choice.

You can set this book aside and return to business as usual, hoping the wave somehow passes you by. It won't. The demographics are certain. The wealth transfer is coming. The only question is whether you're ready.

Or you can act. You can convene your leadership team. You can assess your current capabilities honestly. You can make the case for investment. You can begin the transformation that Estate Readiness requires.

The institutions that act now will capture value for decades. They'll retain deposits that competitors lose. They'll build relationships that span generations. They'll earn reputations that attract families seeking partners, not just providers.

The institutions that wait will wonder what happened. They'll watch wealth walk out the door. They'll struggle to explain shrinking customer bases and aging portfolios. They'll compete for the scraps left by institutions that moved first.

The choice is stark. The opportunity is clear. The time is now.

Final Thoughts

We began this book with a question: What happens on the day your best customer dies?

The answer, we've learned, depends entirely on what happens before that day.

Did you help them prepare? Did you ensure their beneficiary designations reflected their wishes? Did you collect the documents their family would need? Did you introduce yourself to their heirs? Did you build relationships that could survive the transition?

Or did you simply wait, processing transactions, maintaining accounts, taking the relationship for granted, until death revealed the fragility of everything you'd built?

The great wealth transfer will test every financial institution in America. It will separate those who prepared from those who didn't. It will reward relationship depth over transaction volume, multigenerational thinking over quarterly focus, human capability over mere technological efficiency.

Estate Readiness isn't a project. It's not a technology deployment or a process improvement or a training initiative, though it includes all of those. Estate Readiness is a transformation in how you see your purpose, your customers, and your future.

It's the recognition that your most important customers are approaching the end of their lives, and your actions in this chapter will determine whether your institution thrives or merely survives in the next.

It's the commitment to serve families during their most difficult moments with competence and compassion, not because it's profitable (though it is) but because it's right.

It's the investment in human capability alongside technological capability, understanding that no two families are the same, and personalization at scale requires people who can see and respond to each family's unique situation.

It's the long view: building for decades, not quarters; thinking in generations, not years; creating value that compounds over time.

The future of inheritance infrastructure is being written now. The institutions that write it will shape banking for the next generation. They'll set the standard for how financial institutions serve families through life's most consequential transitions.

Will you be among them?

The direction you choose will define your institution for the next two decades. The time is now. The future is waiting.

Estate Readiness Maturity Model

Use this framework to assess your institution's overall Estate Readiness maturity:

Level 1: Reactive

- Estate settlement is purely transactional
- No proactive beneficiary management
- Minimal staff training for estate conversations
- No measurement of estate-related outcomes
- High beneficiary attrition

Level 2: Aware

- Recognition of estate challenge exists
- Some beneficiary designation campaigns
- Basic staff awareness of estate processes
- Limited tracking of estate metrics
- Above-average attrition

Level 3: Developing

- Systematic beneficiary management program
- Staff training on estate conversations
- Technology support for estate processing
- Regular measurement of key metrics
- Average industry retention

Level 4: Proficient

- Integrated estate preparation across customer lifecycle

- Specialized estate team with advanced skills
- Modern infrastructure (digital vault, workflow automation)
- Comprehensive metrics and continuous improvement
- Above-average retention

Level 5: Leading

- Multi-generational relationship model
- Human-AI integration for personalization at scale
- Estate Readiness embedded in institutional culture
- Industry-leading metrics and reputation
- Competitive advantage through estate excellence

Current Level: _____

Target Level (3-Year): _____

Key Gaps to Address:

1.

2.

3.

Book Summary: Key Takeaways

The Challenge

- Trillions in generational wealth transferring through 2048
- 60%+ of inherited wealth leaves within 12 months
- 10,000 Baby Boomers turning 65 daily; deaths rising to 3.6M annually by 2037
- Current systems designed for account holders, not families in transition

The Constraints

- Regulatory complexity across 50+ jurisdictions
- Operational fragmentation (21+ handoffs per estate)
- Technology debt (43% of systems on COBOL)
- Staff unprepared for consequential conversations

The Opportunity

- Estate Readiness: preparation before death, excellence during settlement
- Three pillars: Planning, Documentation, Execution
- Prismm: digital vault and estate orchestration infrastructure
- Trust as competitive moat

The Economics

- 342% five-year ROI potential
- 18-month payback period
- Retention value + efficiency value + relationship value
- Compound effects over time

The Human Dimension

- No two families are the same
- Human capability differentiates when technology is table stakes
- Training, culture, and sustained investment required
- AI enables humans; it doesn't replace them

The Transformation

- Four phases over 36 months

- Executive sponsorship as critical success factor
- Measure leading and lagging indicators
- Integration with broader institutional strategy

The Future

- Gen X receives $39T over next decade; Millennials receive $46T over next 25 years
- Women will control $34T in investable assets by 2030
- Blockchain, AI, digital vaults transform estate infrastructure
- Winners start early, serve whole families, blend tech with humanity

EPILOGUE

A Letter to the Next Generation of Bankers

I wrote this book because I know banking can be better.

Not better in the way that consultants typically mean, more efficient, more profitable, more competitive. Those things matter. But I mean something deeper. I believe banking can be better at serving people during the moments that matter most.

Death is one of those moments. When someone loses a parent, a spouse, a sibling, the last thing they need is an institution that treats them like a problem to process. They need competence, yes, they need accounts transferred, documents filed, assets distributed. But they also need to feel that someone cares. That someone sees them as a person, not a case number.

I've watched families navigate estate settlement with institutions that made everything harder. I've heard stories of widows calling repeatedly for status updates, never reaching the same person twice. I've seen beneficiaries give up and move their inheritance elsewhere: not because they found better rates, but because they couldn't stand dealing with an institution that seemed indifferent to their situation.

I've also seen what's possible when institutions get it right. When a relationship manager calls proactively with clear guidance. When documents are already on file because someone thought ahead. When a family feels genuinely supported through a difficult transition. Those families don't leave. They stay for decades. They tell their friends. They become advocates.

The gap between these two experiences represents the opportunity I've tried to illuminate in this book.

The demographic wave heading toward banking is unprecedented. The numbers are almost too large to comprehend: trillions in wealth changing hands, 10,000 Boomers turning 65 daily, annual deaths climbing toward 4 million. These aren't projections that might happen. They're actuarial certainties unfolding now.

But numbers alone don't capture what this means. Behind every estate is a family. Behind every account transfer is a person who lost someone they loved. Behind every beneficiary designation is a story of relationships, hopes, and intentions that someone wanted to preserve beyond their death.

Banking has always been, at its core, about trust. People trust banks with their money. They trust that deposits will be safe, that payments will process, that accounts will function. This is technical trust, trust in systems and processes.

The great wealth transfer demands a different kind of trust. It demands trust that when a customer dies, their family will be treated with dignity. Trust that wishes documented years ago will be honored. Trust that relationships built over decades will extend to the next generation. This is human trust, trust that the institution cares about people, not just accounts.

Building this kind of trust requires everything I've described in this book: infrastructure that prepares customers before death, processes that serve families efficiently during settlement, technology that enables personalization at scale, and humans who bring judgment and compassion to every interaction.

But mostly, it requires a choice. A choice to see families, not just customers. A choice to prepare, not just process. A choice to invest in capabilities that may not pay off for years. A choice to build something that matters.

I'm often asked whether technology will solve the estate challenge. The honest answer is: both yes and no.

Yes, technology will transform estate operations. AI will extract data from documents automatically. Blockchain may enable self-executing inheritance transfers. Digital vaults will store everything families need. Workflow automation will route cases efficiently. These capabilities will make estate processing faster, cheaper, and more consistent.

But no, technology alone won't solve the challenge. Because the challenge isn't primarily operational. It's relational.

When a widow sits across from a banker to close her husband's accounts, she doesn't need faster processing. She needs someone who acknowledges what she's going through. When siblings disagree about how to handle their parents' estate, they don't need better workflow routing. They need someone who can navigate the family dynamics with wisdom and care. When a son inherits accounts at an institution he's never used, he doesn't need slicker technology. He needs a reason to stay, a sense that this institution served his parents well and will serve him too.

These needs are human. They require human response. The institutions that understand this, that invest in human capability alongside technological capability, will earn trust that technology alone can't create.

I worry sometimes that banking has lost sight of this. In the race to digitize, automate, and optimize, it's easy to forget that behind every transaction is a person with needs that don't fit neatly into digital workflows. The most efficient process in the world still fails if it leaves families feeling processed rather than served.

The institutions that will lead through the great wealth transfer are those that hold both truths simultaneously: efficiency matters AND humanity matters. Technology enables AND people deliver. Speed is important AND presence is essential.

Getting this balance right is the work of the next generation of bankers.

If you're early in your banking career, you will spend your professional life navigating the great wealth transfer. The customers who hold the majority of deposits today will pass those deposits to the next generation during your tenure. How your institution handles this transition will shape its future, and yours.

I hope you'll see this not as a burden but as an opportunity. Few challenges in banking are as consequential. Few offer as much potential for genuine impact. The work of Estate Readiness, helping families prepare, serving them during difficulty, building relationships that span generations, is meaningful work. It's work that matters to real people in real moments.

You'll face pressure to prioritize short-term metrics over long-term relationships. To cut costs in ways that undermine service quality. To automate interactions that should remain human. Resist this pressure when you can. Advocate for investment in capability that compounds. Make the case for approaches that serve families well even when they're harder to measure.

You'll also face moments when you directly impact families during their most difficult transitions. How you show up in those moments, whether you bring competence and compassion or merely process efficiency, will determine whether families remember your institution with gratitude or resentment. Choose to be present. Choose to care. Choose to see the person behind the account.

The great wealth transfer will reward institutions that think in decades, not quarters. It will reward relationship depth over transaction volume. It will reward human capability alongside technological capability. It will reward those who earn trust through consistent, compassionate service over time.

Be part of building that kind of institution.

I want to close with a story.

Early in my career, I watched an elderly woman come into a bank branch after her husband died. She was confused, overwhelmed, carrying a folder of papers she didn't fully understand. She'd been married for 52 years. Her husband had handled all the finances. She didn't know where to start.

The banker who helped her could have processed her paperwork efficiently and moved to the next customer. Instead, he sat with her for over an hour. He explained each document. He helped her understand what would happen next. He gave her his direct phone number and told her to call whenever she had questions. He treated her like his own grandmother.

She didn't move her accounts. Of course she didn't. How could she leave an institution that treated her that way?

That banker understood something essential: banking, at its best, is about serving people during the moments that matter. Efficiency enables that service. Technology supports it. Processes structure it. But humans deliver it.

The great wealth transfer is coming whether we're ready or not. Trillions of dollars will move. Millions of families will navigate loss. The question is what role your institution will play.

Will you be the institution that processes estates efficiently but leaves families feeling like numbers?

Or will you be the institution that families remember with gratitude, the one that helped them prepare, that served them during difficulty, that earned their trust and kept it across generations?

The direction you choose will define your institution for the next two decades. The work starts now.

I know banking can be better. I wrote this book to help you make it so.

Martha Sylla Underwood

APPENDIX

Probate Authority Documents and Estate Processing Reference Guide

This appendix provides a practical reference for the regulatory and procedural landscape discussed throughout this book. It's designed for financial institution executives and operations leaders who want to understand the documentation framework that shapes estate processing at their institutions. This isn't legal advice. It is operational context.

What Are Letters Testamentary and Letters of Administration?

Letters Testamentary and Letters of Administration are court-issued proof-of-authority documents. They show third parties, especially banks and brokerages, who have legal power to act for a deceased person's estate and what that person is authorized to do.

The distinction between the two is straightforward. Letters Testamentary follow a valid will and empower the named executor, the person the deceased chose to handle their affairs. Letters of Administration apply when there is no valid will (a situation called intestacy) or when no executor is available to serve. In that case, the court appoints an administrator.

Both documents serve the same functional purpose: they are portable proof that a specific person has been appointed by a court and that the appointment is current and valid. Financial institutions rely on these documents before releasing funds, disclosing account information, or accepting instructions for accounts titled solely in the deceased's name.

When Letters Are Required, and When They Are Not

Not every death requires Letters. This is a critical point that many families, and some bank employees, do not fully understand. Letters are required for probate-controlled assets, meaning assets titled solely in the deceased's name without a contract-based transfer mechanism. But many modern financial assets pass outside probate entirely through mechanisms built into the account agreement itself.

Assets that typically bypass probate (no Letters required):

Joint accounts with rights of survivorship: the surviving account holder retains access upon presenting a death certificate. Payable-on-death (POD) deposit accounts, sometimes called in-trust-for (ITF) or Totten trust accounts: the bank transfers funds directly to the named beneficiary upon presentation of a death certificate and identification. Transfer-on-death (TOD) securities registrations: similar to POD, but for brokerage and investment accounts. Trust-held accounts: the successor trustee named in the trust document takes over upon presenting a death certificate and trustee certification.

Assets that typically require probate authority (Letters needed):

Accounts titled solely in the deceased's name with no beneficiary designation on file. Accounts where the named beneficiary has predeceased the account holder or is listed as "estate of" the deceased. Accounts with disputed ownership, unclear titling, or ambiguous beneficiary records.

This distinction explains a significant portion of the friction families experience. When beneficiary designations are complete and current, accounts transfer with minimal delay. When they are not, the estate must go through probate, and the institution must wait for court-issued authority before acting. This is exactly why the beneficiary designation campaigns described in Chapter 8 represent the highest-leverage intervention available to any institution pursuing Estate Readiness.

Why Financial Institutions Request Letters

From the institution's perspective, the rationale is grounded in three operational realities:

Fraud prevention. Death certificates can be counterfeited. Wills can be fabricated. Letters Testamentary can be altered. Court stamps can be faked. Every document in the estate process represents a potential point of fraud. The institution needs court-verified credentials before releasing significant assets.

Liability protection. If a bank releases funds to the wrong person, whether through fraud or inadequate verification, it can be held liable to the rightful heirs for the full amount plus damages. Courts have held banks liable even when they relied on apparently valid documents, if they failed to exercise reasonable care.

Regulatory compliance. Federal anti-money laundering rules require identity verification for anyone taking control of funds. The beneficiary, even if they're the deceased's own child, is a new person to the bank's compliance systems and must be verified accordingly.

This isn't bureaucratic obstinacy. It's risk management in an environment where estate fraud costs billions annually and a single wrongful release can generate regulatory scrutiny, litigation, and reputational damage that far exceeds the value of the account in question.

Small Estate Shortcuts: When Full Probate Is Not Required

Many states provide simplified procedures for smaller estates that reduce or eliminate the need for full probate and formal Letters. These shortcuts are underutilized because most families do not know they exist, and many bank employees are not trained to recognize when they apply.

Two common patterns exist across states:

Affidavit or declaration collection: Used for personal property below a state-defined threshold. The executor or heir signs a sworn statement, sometimes notarized, sometimes filed with the court, and presents it to the institution in lieu of full probate documents.

Summary administration: A court-supervised shortcut for estates below a higher threshold. Faster and less expensive than full probate, but still involves court oversight.

Selected State Thresholds for Small Estate Procedures (Illustrative)

Note: These thresholds are examples for orientation purposes. They're periodically updated by state legislatures and should be confirmed against current state law before relying on them operationally.

California: Small estate affidavit for personal property valued under $208,850 (for deaths on or after April 1, 2025). Requires at least 40 days to have passed after death. Simplified procedure for primary residences valued up to $750,000.

New York: Voluntary administration (small estate) for personal property with gross value of $50,000 or less, subject to statutory exclusions. The Surrogate's Court issues certificates for each asset that the voluntary administrator uses to collect property.

Florida: Summary administration permitted when the estate subject to administration (less exempt property) doesn't exceed $75,000, or when the deceased has been dead for more than two years.

Texas: Small estate affidavit available for intestate estates with limited debts and estate assets (excluding homestead and exempt property) not exceeding $75,000.

These thresholds matter operationally because a family inheriting a $60,000 account faces a dramatically different process depending solely on which state's laws apply. An institution operating across multiple states must train staff to recognize when small estate shortcuts are available and guide families accordingly.

How Financial Institutions Process Death Claims: A Decision Framework

When a death notification arrives, the institution's response follows a decision path based on how the asset is titled in its records. Understanding this path helps explain why processing takes the time it does, and where opportunities for improvement exist.

Step 1: Verify the death. The institution requires a certified death certificate. This is universal across all account types and all institutions.

Step 2: Determine how the asset is titled. Is it a joint account with survivorship rights? Is it a trust-held account? Does it have a payable-on-death or transfer-on-death beneficiary on file? Or is it solely owned with no beneficiary designation?

Step 3: Follow the appropriate processing path.

For joint accounts with survivorship: The surviving owner retains access. The institution removes the deceased from the account upon receiving the death certificate. This is typically the fastest resolution.

For accounts with verified beneficiaries (POD, TOD, ITF): The beneficiary completes claim forms and provides identification. The institution transfers funds according to the account agreement. No court documents required.

For trust-titled accounts: The successor trustee presents a death certificate and trustee certification naming them as the new trustee. The institution may request relevant pages of the trust document.

For solely owned accounts with no beneficiary: This is where full probate authority enters the picture. The institution requires either court-issued Letters Testamentary or Letters of Administration, a qualifying small estate affidavit, or a specific court order directing release. No activity occurs on the account until legal authority is established.

Step 4: Document review and processing. Once documents are received, the institution reviews them against its internal requirements. A major bank's published guidance asks customers to allow ten business days after document receipt for review. Some institutions require original or recently certified documents. Documents may be rejected if they are outdated, missing the appropriate court seal, or signed in the wrong capacity.

Typical Documentation Requirements by Account Type

For solely owned deposit accounts without a beneficiary: Certified death certificate (multiple copies recommended), Letters Testamentary or Letters of Administration from the probate court (or qualifying small estate affidavit), government-issued photo identification for the executor or administrator, Employer Identification Number (EIN) for the estate if an estate account is being opened, and institution-specific forms such as letters of instruction or signature cards.

For payable-on-death or transfer-on-death accounts: Certified death certificate, beneficiary identification (government-issued photo ID), and institution claim or letter-of-instruction forms.

For brokerage accounts: Documentation requirements are often broader and may include death certificate, court letter of appointment (current date, visible or original court seal), affidavit of domicile, tax waiver if applicable, and letters of authorization for certain transfers based on account form and survivorship facts.

Document Validity and Common Rejection Issues

A frequent source of frustration for families is document rejection. Many disputes between families and financial institutions are actually document-matching problems, not disputes over the executor's legitimacy. Common reasons for rejection include:

The court document is outdated. Some institutions require documents dated within a specific window. In at least one jurisdiction, certificates of letters are explicitly valid for only six months.

The court seal is missing or illegible. Institutions require visible, original court seals on probate documents.

The document is signed in the wrong capacity. An executor presenting documents in their personal capacity rather than their fiduciary capacity may be rejected.

The document type does not match the institution's requirements. Different states issue different forms of appointment documentation. What one state calls Letters Testamentary, another may call a Certificate of Appointment or Short Certificate.

For institutions pursuing Estate Readiness, training frontline staff to understand these rejection patterns, and to communicate requirements clearly and completely at first contact, eliminates a significant source of processing delay and family frustration.

A Note on Using This Reference

This appendix consolidates publicly available regulatory and procedural information for operational reference. It doesn't constitute legal advice. State laws change, institution policies vary, and individual circumstances require individual analysis. The value of this reference is in providing your leadership team with a working vocabulary for the regulatory landscape that shapes estate processing, so that conversations about improvement can be grounded in how the system actually works rather than how we assume it works.

For institution-specific guidance, consult your compliance and legal teams. For state-specific questions, refer to the relevant state probate code and your state banking department's published guidance.

NOTES AND SOURCES

The research, data, and institutional references cited throughout this book are compiled here for reference. Sources are organized by the chapter in which they first appear.

Sources and Citations

Demographic Data:

- U.S. Census Bureau, "By 2030, All Baby Boomers Will Be Age 65 or Older," December 2019. Since 2011, approximately 10,000 Boomers have crossed the age-65 threshold daily.
- U.S. Census Bureau, "Demographic Turning Points for the United States: Population Projections," March 2020.
- National Center for Health Statistics, National Vital Statistics System: The United States experiences approximately 2.8 million deaths annually. Mortality data shows deaths projected to rise to 3.6 million by 2037 and peak around 2055 as Boomers age through peak mortality years.
- Congressional Budget Office, "The Demographic Outlook: 2026 to 2056," January 2026. Beginning in 2030, annual deaths are projected to exceed annual births.

Wealth Transfer Data:

- Cerulli Associates, "The Cerulli Report. U.S. High-Net-Worth and Ultra-High-Net-Worth Markets 2024," December 2024. Projects $124 trillion in wealth transfers through 2048, with $105 trillion flowing to heirs and $18 trillion to charity. Nearly $100 trillion will transfer from Baby Boomers and older generations (81% of all transfers). Millennials projected to inherit $46 trillion; Gen X to receive $39 trillion.

Beneficiary Experience:

- Composite narrative based on documented estate settlement processes. Timelines reflect typical probate duration of 6-12 months for moderately complex estates. Processing steps derived from FDIC guidance on deceased account procedures and industry standard practices as documented by American Bankers Association.

Note: The story of Margaret and Jennifer Chen is a composite illustration based on common patterns in estate settlement. Names and specific details are fictional. The systemic challenges depicted reflect documented industry practices.

Sources and Citations

Probate Timelines:

- American Bar Association: Average probate duration is 6-9 months for typical estates; complex estates may take several years.
- FindLaw: Summary probate can complete in as few as 4 months; typical estate administration may take up to 2 years.
- LegalZoom: Standard probate takes 6-12 months; California probate typically takes 9-18 months with mandatory 4-month creditor claim period.

Letters Testamentary:

- Trust & Will: Letters Testamentary grant an executor legal authority to act on behalf of the estate; required to access bank accounts, transfer property, and handle financial matters.
- MetLife: Financial institutions require Letters Testamentary to show legal authority to access accounts of the deceased.

Small Estate Thresholds (Examples as of 2025):

- California: $208,850 for personal property (Small Estate Affidavit); $750,000 for primary residence (simplified procedure)
- Texas: $75,000 (small estate affidavit)
- New York: $50,000 (voluntary administration) Note: Thresholds vary significantly by state and are periodically adjusted for inflation.

Documentation Requirements:

- Bank of America Estate Services: Required documents typically include death certificate, Letters Testamentary or Letters of Administration, executor identification, and estate tax identification number.

Note: The story of Sarah Martinez is a composite illustration based on common patterns in estate settlement. Names and specific details are fictional. The procedural challenges depicted reflect documented industry practices and regulatory requirements.

Sources and Citations

Beneficiary Attrition Data:

- CREALOGIX: "80% of clients change advisors at the point of inheritance.. Despite the major risk, 76% of firms only engage with heirs at the point of transfer."
- McKinsey: "70 percent of women switch their wealth relationship to a new financial institution within a year of their spouse's death."
- Natixis Investment Managers 2024 Global Survey: "U.S. advisors report retaining client relationships 78% of the time when the spouse inherits. But when the children inherit the assets, that retention level drops to 58%."

Existential Threat:

- Natixis Investment Managers: "46% of financial advisors worldwide say the Great Wealth Transfer represents an 'existential threat' to their business."

Wealth Transfer Scale:

- Cerulli Associates: "$124 trillion will transfer to heirs and charity through 2048."
- Citizens Bank: "Despite the importance of these decisions and the historic wealth transfer anticipated over the coming decades, many individuals have yet to establish a formal plan. In fact, only 24% of adults reported having a will (or revocable trust) in 2025."

Industry Response:

- State Street Global Advisors: "38% of investors retain the same advisor when their spouse dies. And that number drops to 29% when both parents have passed away and children inherit their assets."
- Accenture: "81% of advisors hold meetings to help clients navigate complicated family dynamics."

Sources and Citations

State Probate Variations:

- FindLaw, "State Laws: Estates and Probate": State laws about estates, creating wills, property distribution and probate administration are governed by each state's specific codes.
- LegalMatch, "How Does the Probate Process Vary From State to State?": The probate process varies from state to state due to differences in laws and regulations.

Community Property States:

- Nolo.com, "Property Ownership Rules in Marriage": Nine states follow community property rules; the remaining 41 follow common law property rules.
- Trust & Will: The nine community property states are Arizona, California, Idaho, Louisiana, Nevada, New Mexico, Texas, Washington, and Wisconsin.

KYC/AML Requirements:

- FinCEN and regulatory guidance: KYC procedures are required under the Bank Secrecy Act and USA PATRIOT Act.
- Trulioo, "AML and KYC Requirements for Banking": Customer identification and verification is a core component of AML compliance.

FDIC/NCUA Grace Period:

- NCUA FAQ: The NCUA will insure a deceased member's accounts as if he or she were still alive for six months after death.
- FDIC provides similar six-month grace period for deposit insurance coverage.

Fiduciary Liability:

- Justia, "Executor's Breach of Fiduciary Duty": An executor has a fiduciary duty to always act in the best interest of the estate.
- Keystone Law: If an executor's actions fail to align with beneficiary interests, they may constitute executor misconduct.

Small Estate Thresholds:

- California Courts (DE-300): Small Estate Affidavit threshold of $208,850 effective April 2025.
- State thresholds vary from approximately $10,000 to over $200,000.

Sources and Citations

Organizational Silos:

- Boston Consulting Group: "In siloed organizations, as much as 15% of total workforce capacity is consumed by redundant activities that exist solely because information and processes don't flow effectively across departmental boundaries."
- Banking Dive: "Customer context gets lost in translation between departments, forcing clients to repeat information and creating friction at every transition point."

Branch Training Challenges:

- Wells Fargo (Computer Weekly): "Banking staff at branches typically dealt with only one bereavement a month, which meant they did not always have the specialist knowledge to manage the client's financial estate."

Technology Integration:

- Wells Fargo Estate Care Centre: Implemented Pega workflow automation to create unified case files and coordinate across departments, enabling staff to pick up cases without requiring families to repeat their story.
- American Banker: "The foundation starts with common definitions on what constitutes an authoritative death notification, who is authorized to act at each stage of the process and which documents establish that authority."

System Fragmentation:

- Latinia: "Data silos occur due to various factors, including organizational structure, legacy systems, departmental autonomy, and lack of data governance."
- TTEC Digital: "The silos that tend to hurt the customer and member experience most are the data and technology silos that exist within individual departments, making it almost impossible for relevant customer information to pass from one system to another."

Sources and Citations

COBOL and Mainframe Statistics:

- Reuters: 43% of US banking core systems built on COBOL; COBOL programmers aged 45-55 years old
- Industry analysts: 220 billion lines of COBOL in operation worldwide
- Phil Teplitzky study: Average age of COBOL programmer is 58, with 10% retiring annually; estimated 84,000 unfilled mainframe positions
- COBOL processes 95% of ATM transactions and 80% of in-person banking transactions

IT Budget Allocation:

- Industry research: Banks spend 60-80% of IT budgets on maintaining existing systems
- RS2 white paper: Banks spend up to 70 cents of every IT dollar on legacy maintenance
- Credit unions reportedly spend approximately 90% of technology budgets on legacy and existing systems maintenance
- McKinsey: Only 5-10 cents of every technology dollar delivers actual business value
- Deloitte survey: Average enterprise spends 57% of IT budget on supporting business operations, only 16% on innovation

Technology Debt Impact:

- McKinsey survey of CIOs: Companies pay an additional 10-20% to address tech debt on top of any project costs
- About 30% of CIOs believe more than 20% of their technical budget allocated to new products is diverted to resolving tech debt issues
- Banks need 6-18 months to launch new offerings vs. 2-3 months for digital-first competitors
- Only 32% of banks have successfully integrated AI into their core systems

Core System Challenges:

- Many core banking systems still run on COBOL, a programming language designed in 1959
- Accrevent: The shrinking pool of COBOL developers due to retirement means banks are running code without fully understanding its function
- Commonwealth Bank of Australia: Core system replacement took five years and cost approximately $750 million
- American Bankers Association 2024 Survey: 35% of US banks are dissatisfied with their current core processor

Spaghetti Architecture:

- Banks describe their technology landscapes as "spaghetti tree" architecture due to convoluted interdependencies built up over decades
- Point-to-point integrations accumulate over time, creating brittle architectures

Modernization Approaches:

- Endava 2024 Retail Banking Report: 47% of banks pursue incremental change; 40% pursue progressive modernization; 13% choose total replacement
- Wells Fargo implemented Pegasystems workflow software to coordinate estate processing across legacy systems
- API layers can "wrap" legacy systems to expose modern interfaces without replacing underlying infrastructure

Sources and Citations

Wealth Transfer Statistics:

- Cerulli Associates: $84 trillion will be transferred through 2045
- Cerulli Associates: 89% of high-net-worth firms cite family-focused services as a top growth strategy

Estate Planning Gaps:

- Research indicates only approximately 32% of Americans have an estate plan
- Without proper planning, wealth may be lost to taxes, legal fees, or family disputes

Beneficiary Designations:

- POD/TOD designations allow accounts to bypass probate and transfer directly to beneficiaries
- Accounts with beneficiary designations transfer upon presentation of death certificate and identification, without court documents

Multi-Generational Engagement:

- State Street: "Many clients put off thinking about wealth transfer plans until an emergency forces the conversation. But by then, it may be too late."
- T. Rowe Price: Advisors who build meaningful relationships with heirs retain significantly more assets when wealth transfers occur
- Industry research: Firms with multi-generational engagement strategies retain 70-80% of inherited assets vs. 30-40% for firms without such strategies

Three Pillars Framework:

- Planning, Documentation, and Execution pillars address the constraints identified in Chapters 4-6
- Purpose-built inheritance infrastructure provides integrated capabilities without requiring core system replacement
- The infrastructure approach leverages trust relationships while addressing technology debt constraints

Sources and Citations

Transformation Success Rates:

- Research indicates that approximately 70% of transformation initiatives fail to achieve their intended objectives
- McKinsey research shows that organizations fully implementing defined health-improvement measures see nearly double the returns of those that don't

Executive Sponsorship:

- Prosci research identifies effective executive sponsorship as the greatest contributor to successful change across all nine of their benchmarking studies
- When asked to identify the biggest obstacle to success, participants identified lack of executive support and active sponsorship as their primary obstacle

Change Management:

- Research shows that organizations providing continuous reinforcement see adoption rates 40% higher than those relying on launch-day training alone
- Employees are 4x more likely to trust change messages from their direct manager than from corporate communications

Implementation Best Practices:

- Pilot programs help identify potential issues early and avoid the high failure rates associated with full-scale system overhauls
- Phased rollouts allow organizations to gain insights into performance, user experience, and potential areas for improvement during earlier phases

ROI Timeline:

- BCG research suggests transformation initiatives require 12-18 months for meaningful ROI in comprehensive implementations
- Deloitte research indicates transformation projects should plan for 12-24 months for comprehensive value realization

Community Bank/Credit Union Transformation:

- Research shows that digitally mature credit unions experience up to 2x the annual revenue growth compared to less tech-savvy counterparts
- Financial institutions embracing digital platforms experience up to 20% increase in customer satisfaction compared to those relying solely on traditional methods

Sources and Citations

Customer Experience Impact:

- Research indicates banks with superior customer experience see 50% higher customer retention rates and 20% increase in cross-sell opportunities

- Customer experience is increasingly viewed as the primary competitive battleground in financial services

Retention Economics:

- Increasing customer retention by 5% can increase profits by 25% to 95%
- Acquiring new customers costs 5-7 times more than retaining existing ones
- U.S. retail banks lose an estimated 12-15% of customers annually

Relationship Deepening:

- After one purchase, customers return approximately 25% of the time
- After two purchases, the likelihood nearly doubles
- After three purchases, return likelihood reaches approximately 62%
- Businesses have 60-70% chance of selling to existing customers vs. 5-20% for new prospects

Cross-Sell and Lifetime Value:

- Customer lifetime value commonly doubles for customers positively impacted by effective cross-sell programs
- Average American has 5.3 bank accounts; many have 30-40 financial relationships
- Share of wallet competition has intensified as customers fragment across providers

Multigenerational Strategy:

- Cerulli Associates: 89% of high-net-worth firms cite family-focused services as top growth strategy
- More than $84 trillion projected to transfer to heirs through 2045, with nearly half flowing to Millennials and Gen Z
- Engaging heirs during client lifetimes significantly improves asset retention at wealth transfer

Fintech Competition:

- Neobanks and challenger banks have intensified competition through superior digital experience
- Traditional banks maintain advantages in trust, stability, and relationship-intensive services
- 74% of new bank accounts in 2025 opened online; digital-only banks account for 22% of new accounts

Sources and Citations

Banking Economics:

- Net interest income represents the spread between interest earned on loans and interest paid on deposits

- Net interest margin for community banks typically ranges from 2.5% to 4.0%
- Customer retention improvements of 5% can increase profits by 25% to 95%

Operational Costs:

- Estate processing typically requires 7-8 hours of staff time per case across multiple departments
- Fully loaded labor costs (including benefits and overhead) average $40-55 per hour for operations staff
- Processing efficiency improvements of 40-50% are achievable through workflow automation and document pre-collection

Customer Acquisition vs. Retention:

- Customer acquisition costs in banking range from $300-500 per new relationship
- Retention is 5-7 times more cost-effective than acquisition
- Average customer relationship length targets of 7+ years justify long-term retention investment

Technology Investment ROI:

- Financial institutions typically require 15-25% annual ROI for technology investments
- Transformation projects require 12-24 months for meaningful value realization
- Phased implementation reduces risk and enables learning before full deployment

Deposit Value:

- Deposits fund lending activities, making retention directly connected to lending capacity
- Net interest income is the primary profitability metric for retail banking
- Retained deposits generate recurring value through ongoing net interest margin

Sources and Citations

Emotional Intelligence and Empathy Training:

- Research shows structured empathy training improves emotional intelligence with effect sizes between 0.44-0.58
- Companies investing in empathy training see CSAT improvements of 15-25%, employee retention increases of 25-50%
- TalentSmart research found that 90% of top performers have high emotional intelligence
- Continuous coaching leads to 15-25% rise in customer satisfaction scores

Compassion Fatigue:

- Cornell study found 87% of workers report high stress levels in customer-facing roles, 77% report high personal stress

- Frequent exposure to others' hardships can lead to compassion fatigue characterized by cynicism and emotional exhaustion
- Recognizing and addressing compassion fatigue requires ongoing organizational support

AI and Human Balance:

- 80% of routine banking tasks can now be automated through AI
- 72% of banking customers would consider returning to banks providing more human-like, empathetic interactions
- AI-powered chatbots can resolve up to 80% of routine inquiries without human intervention
- Banks implementing human-AI partnerships report 15% reductions in handling times with improved satisfaction

Bereavement Training:

- Hospice organizations typically provide 20-30 hours of initial bereavement training including grief education, communication skills, and role-playing
- Certified bereavement coordinators require bachelor's degree plus continuing education and supervised experience
- "Companioning" approach emphasizes being present rather than treating, walking alongside rather than leading

Personalization at Scale:

- Banks using AI to surface insights while training staff to translate into human connections outperform
- Continuous personalization through AI tools helping frontline staff in real-time shows improved outcomes
- 40% higher adoption of desired behaviors with continuous reinforcement versus one-time training

Sources and Citations

Wealth Transfer Projections:

- Cerulli Associates: Generational wealth transfer projections through 2048
- Gen X projected to inherit $39 trillion; Millennials $46 trillion
- Baby Boomers and older Americans responsible for $79 trillion in transfers
- Approximately 50% of transfers from top 2% of households

Generational Characteristics:

- Gen X lost 38% of median net worth between 2007-2010
- 87% of children plan to take management of inheritance elsewhere

- By 2030, 80% of new wealth management clients will want Netflix-style digital engagement
- 70% of wealthy families lose wealth by second generation; 90% by third

Women and Wealth:

- Women will control $34 trillion in investable assets by 2030
- $40 trillion expected to pass to widowed women
- 84% of women lack confidence managing inheritance (vs. 73% of men)
- $9 trillion expected to pass "sideways" to female partners

Demographic Trends:

- Nearly half of current relationship managers expected to retire by 2040
- Gen Z expected to have $36 trillion income by 2030, $74 trillion by 2040
- Gen Z share of millennial/Gen Z clients at HNW firms grew from 8% (2021) to 25% (2024)

Technology Evolution:

- Smart contracts can automate inheritance transfers upon verified conditions
- Blockchain provides tamper-proof records for estate documents
- Digital asset inheritance requires new solutions (cryptocurrency, NFTs)
- Legal frameworks for blockchain-based inheritance still evolving

Regulatory Changes:

- California AB 2016: Simplified probate for primary residences up to $750,000 (effective April 2025)
- India Banking Laws Amendment Act 2025: Expanded nomination to four nominees
- Federal estate tax exemption scheduled to drop to ~$7M in 2026
- SECURE Act requires inherited retirement accounts distributed within 10 years

Sources and Citations

Wealth Transfer Projections:

- Cerulli Associates: Generational wealth transfer projections through 2048
- Gen X projected to inherit $39 trillion; Millennials $46 trillion
- Baby Boomers and older Americans responsible for $79 trillion in transfers
- Approximately 50% of transfers from top 2% of households

Generational Characteristics:

- Gen X lost 38% of median net worth between 2007-2010
- 87% of children plan to take management of inheritance elsewhere

- By 2030, 80% of new wealth management clients will want Netflix-style digital engagement
- 70% of wealthy families lose wealth by second generation; 90% by third

Women and Wealth:

- Women will control $34 trillion in investable assets by 2030
- $40 trillion expected to pass to widowed women
- 84% of women lack confidence managing inheritance (vs. 73% of men)
- $9 trillion expected to pass "sideways" to female partners

Demographic Trends:

- Nearly half of current relationship managers expected to retire by 2040
- Gen Z expected to have $36 trillion income by 2030, $74 trillion by 2040
- Gen Z share of millennial/Gen Z clients at HNW firms grew from 8% (2021) to 25% (2024)

Technology Evolution:

- Smart contracts can automate inheritance transfers upon verified conditions
- Blockchain provides tamper-proof records for estate documents
- Digital asset inheritance requires new solutions (cryptocurrency, NFTs)
- Legal frameworks for blockchain-based inheritance still evolving

Regulatory Changes:

- California AB 2016: Simplified probate for primary residences up to $750,000 (effective April 2025)
- India Banking Laws Amendment Act 2025: Expanded nomination to four nominees
- Federal estate tax exemption scheduled to drop to ~$7M in 2026
- SECURE Act requires inherited retirement accounts distributed within 10 years

www.ingramcontent.com/pod-product-compliance
Lightning Source LLC
LaVergne TN
LVHW010057110826
845155LV00028B/385

* 9 7 8 1 9 5 3 6 5 3 2 0 8 *